Reader's Digest · National Trust

Nature Notebooks

ORNAMENTAL TREES

Reader's Digest · National Trust

Nature Notebooks

ORNAMENTAL TREES

Published by The Reader's Digest Association Limited, London,
in association with The National Trust

Additional editorial work by Duncan Petersen Publishing Ltd.
5 Botts Mews, London W2 5AG.
Typesetting by Modern Reprographics Ltd., Hull, North Humberside.
Separations by Modern Reprographics Ltd. (covers)
and Mullis Morgan Ltd., London (duplicate film).
Printed by Everbest Printing Company Ltd., Hong Kong.

The illustration on the cover is of Sheffield Park Garden
by Michael Woods.

CONTENTS

Using This Book	6-7
Basic Fieldcraft	8-10
The Trees	11-95
The Sites	96-124
Glossary	125
Index	126
Acknowledgements	128

Using this book

The British Isles are host to a wonderful variety of ornamental trees and it is everyone's good fortune that of these all the most interesting types can be seen on National Trust properties.

This book takes advantage of that happy coincidence by being not only a field guide to ornamental trees, but also a gazetteer of National Trust sites where there is every opportunity to see the species, indeed not just to see them, but to observe some of the finest specimens of their kind. Because the National Trust manages its property (see opposite) and because public access is almost always easy, making a special journey to any of the sites is indeed worthwhile.

The page references
In a box on each colour plate page in the field guide section you will find a brief general note on each species and then a sequence of numbers, and it is these which are the key to the book's dual function as identification guide and sites gazetteer. The references simply direct you to sites where you will see the species in question. They are not the only sites listed where you can see that species; but they are ones which the book's editor has singled out as being especially worth a visit for that species in particular; often the sites boast especially large, or beautiful examples of the tree or shrub in question; often, too, they will be among the select few places in the British Isles where a rare species can be seen. Equally, you will find some species cross-referenced to a site, but not mentioned in the site description: this is because space in the gazetteer is restricted.

Choice of species
Illustrated in the field guide section on pages 12-95 are the most likely trees to be seen on property of the National Trust, the National Trust for Scotland, or in one of the Republic of Ireland's main national tree collections. The book features a very few essentially well-known ornamental trees (eg Horse Chestnut and laburnum) to allow for the inclusion of some trees that are less well-known but extremely attractive.

In each property entry, only a sample number of trees has been mentioned as, inevitably, all the trees growing on a property could not be comprehensively listed. However, most trees illustrated in the field guide section are listed, together with those that are particularly important to that property (for example, eucryphias at Nymans). Also singled out for mention are cultivars or forms of trees illustrated in the companion volume in the *Nature Notebooks* series, *Woodland Trees*. Where a tree could be planted either for ornament or for its timber (for example walnut), it is mentioned in the text of both books but is illustrated only in *Woodland Trees*.

In order to list as many trees as possible on a property, each tree tends to be mentioned only once, even if it appears in several other places in that garden or park. The nomenclature used is that appearing in the Reader's Digest *Field Guide to Trees and Shrubs of Britain*.

The 'notebook' panels
Making records of field observations is an excellent habit: it makes identification easier the next time round if you stop to think about, and record, the features which enabled you to name a species; and it will bring back happy memories of days out. The space left blank for your notes at the foot of each page is intended as an introduction to making field notes; many will want to develop it further by buying a full-size notebook. Perhaps the most important section of the notebook panel is that left blank for sketches: however amateur you may think your efforts in this direction, they *are* worth making, for a drawing, however feeble, forces you to observe in detail.

Further advice on record-making, and tips on basic fieldcraft – how to set about identifying ornamental trees – is given on pages 8-10.

Help for visitors
Many of the National Trust's ornamental trees grow in parks and gardens where expert staff are on hand to answer queries and guide visitors to the specimens they want to see. An added bonus may also be the presence of well-signposted nature walks designed to take you round the key features of the property; and of course, there are also likely to be such amenities as car parks, information centres and tea rooms.

Choice of sites
Every site featured in the gazetteer section has been chosen in conjunction with a top horticultural expert to give an interesting and representative cross-section of Trust properties. A significant portion are sites which are readily accessible from major centres of population, or which are in parts of the country particularly popular for holidays.

Opening hours and admissions

The times of opening, and the admission fees are those which were current at time of going to press. The National Trust and the National Trust for Scotland review their admission fees each year, so that in general there is the possibility of a modest increase over the sum stated. Full information on opening hours and admission fees is published in the following annual publications: *National Trust Properties Open,* the National Trust for Scotland's *Guide to over 100 Properties,* and the Historic Irish Tourist Houses and Gardens Association's *Houses, Castles and Gardens Open to the Public.*

A large number of the National Trust properties in this book comprise an historic house and grounds; prices given generally refer to admission to both house and grounds, but in some cases special arrangements are available for those who wish to enter the grounds only.

TREES FOR ORNAMENT – THE WORK OF THE NATIONAL TRUST

The National Trust's gardens reflect the enormous richness and variety of the British tree collection tradition and together constitute the greatest collection of ornamental trees owned by a single private organization.

John Veitch, who began Britain's most influential-ever tree nursery and sponsored many collectors, started his career with Sir Thomas Acland at Killerton near Exeter in Devon in the late eighteenth century. (The garden there contains some of this original introductions.) Now the National Trust is reintroducing many of the species first brought into cultivation by the house of Veitch, where possible using wild seeds again.

New blood of this kind both widens the genetic base of each species and restores authentic material where species have become mixed by hybridising.

Many of our most beautiful trees have been produced, accidentally or deliberately, in cultivation by selection or by crossing one wild species with another to produce a cultivar. Over the years, nurserymen and amateurs have had much profit and pleasure from producing new and 'improved' cultivars by these and other means. Where National Trust gardens such as Trelissick in Cornwall and Powis Castle in Welshpool, Powys,

have a tradition for planting the often more showy cultivars in preference to true species from the wild, the practice is continued. Gardens should not and cannot remain static and the Trust tries to continue to develop each collection in the way that the former owner might have done.

Despite a continued and heartening increase of interest in trees and gardens generally, the range of plants readily available in nurseries has been drastically narrowed in recent years in response to economic pressure and the spread of garden centres, where plants are sold principally on their immediate impact. In its endeavour to maintain standards, the Trust keeps in touch with nurseries nationally and internationally and runs its own small nursery.

Depending on taste, almost any tree can be described as ornamental whether or not normally used as a specimen tree in a garden or park. What could be more beautiful than the magnificent beeches at Stourhead, the wind-blown sycamores at Felbrigg, Norfolk, and the towering oaks at Powis Castle? Yet these are usually termed forest trees and it is right that these native and traditional trees – green in leaf, firm and rounded in habit – should usually form the structure among which the showier and more exotic kinds

can be seen to best effect. In larger gardens oak, beech, lime, chestnut, hornbeam and ash (but sadly no longer elm), form the boundary shelter belts, the background plantings and the avenues that hold the layout together.

A long-term strategy, consistently pursued, is essential for the conservation of gardens, especially where trees are concerned. With its stability and continuity of purpose, the National Trust is well qualified for this role. Whether in gardens, arboreta or landscape parks, a continuous and gradual programme of renewal, felling and replanting is necessary so as to anticipate, by several years, inevitable losses and so as to achieve a balance of ages. Considerable knowledge, experience and imagination are needed to visualize the ultimate impact of every newly planted tree when eventually it matures.

At its highest level, growing trees for ornament demands a wide range of qualities – foresight and imagination; aesthetic sensitivity; sense of history; consistency with flexibility; horticultural knowledge and practical skill. Not surprising then that it has become the abiding interest of so many great men.

John Gales
Gardens Adviser, The National Trust

Basic Fieldcraft

KEY TO BROAD-LEAVED TREES

The trees and shrubs illustrated and described in the main part of this book have been grouped according to the shape of their leaves; for throughout most of the year this provides the single most obvious clue by which to identify them. When trying to put a name to a tree or shrub, first compare its leaves with those illustrated in this key.

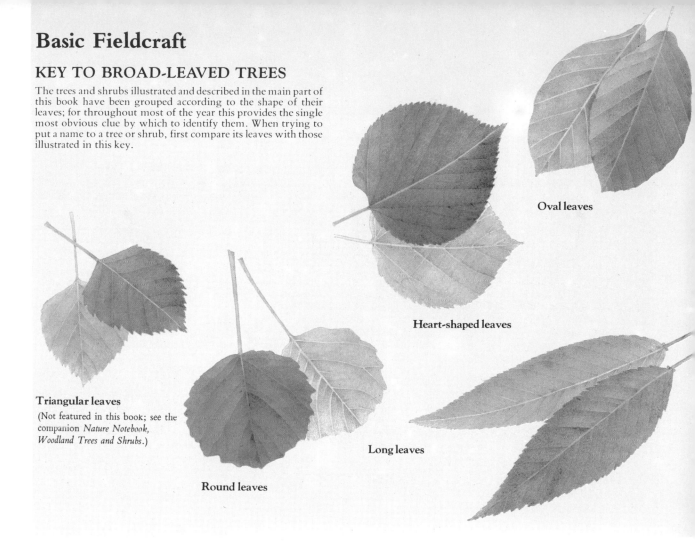

Oval leaves

Heart-shaped leaves

Triangular leaves
(Not featured in this book; see the companion *Nature Notebook, Woodland Trees and Shrubs*.)

Long leaves

Round leaves

If there is one failsafe piece of advice for the would-be naturalist, it is never to try to learn too much at once. This holds particularly true for those who want to identify, and observe trees for, unlike birds and insects, they have the advantage of not rushing about. There is all the time in the world to study them.

Absolutely basic to successful tree identification is a notebook, or a space for notes, such as provided in this book, and a sharp pencil. If you have a camera, take that along too. Notes are essential because, although you may think you can remember all the necessary details, it is amazing how quickly they become blurred. If you can make a few sketches, they should help, as will photographs.

Once confronted by your chosen tree what you look for to assist identification will largely be determined by the time of year; which is why the panel left blank in the *Nature Notebook* has a space specifically for the date. However, a useful first step, no matter what the season, is to take an overall look. Note the height and general shape (remembering that if a tree is closely surrounded by others this will affect its growth and shape).

Next consider whether your tree is broad-leaved or coniferous. Most broad-leaved trees shed their leaves in winter –

Maple-like leaves

Hand-shaped leaves

Feather-like leaves

Lobed leaves

Unusual leaves

in other words, they are deciduous. The leaves of conifers are either needle-like or small and scale-like, and mostly evergreen. Notable exceptions to this rule are holly and larch. The fact that most coniferous trees are evergreen means that you are looking for more or less the same basic clues to identification all the year round: if it has needles, are they long or short and are they grouped in twos, threes or more? Are they hard or soft, dark or pale green? If a conifer has small, hard leaves, note their arrangement, texture and colour. Are they in opposite pairs or alternate? Are they, for example, bright green, yellowish or dark green? Crush some of the foliage and try to remember the smell. It can be most distinctive. Are there any flowers on the tree, and if so, what are they like? The general appearance of the cones can also help.

Again, all these factors will, with the help of the field guide pages in this book, narrow down the range of possible identifications.

If your tree is broad-leaved, make a special point of examining the twigs and leaf buds in winter and early spring. See whether the twigs are straight or angled, rough or smooth. Are the leaf buds opposite each other, alternate or even in a spiral? Note their shape, colour and

KEY TO CONIFEROUS TREES

The leaves of coniferous trees can be divided into those which are needle-like and those which resemble scales. Trees with scale-like leaves sometimes also have awl-shaped juvenile leaves which persist on the adult tree. The needle-like leaves fall into four groups. Pines have long needles in groups of two, three or five. Spruce needles are sharp and arise on pegs. The needles of cedars and larches are in rosettes on the older twigs; those of larches are deciduous. Other trees have flat needles, including the silver firs whose needles leave a round leaf scar.

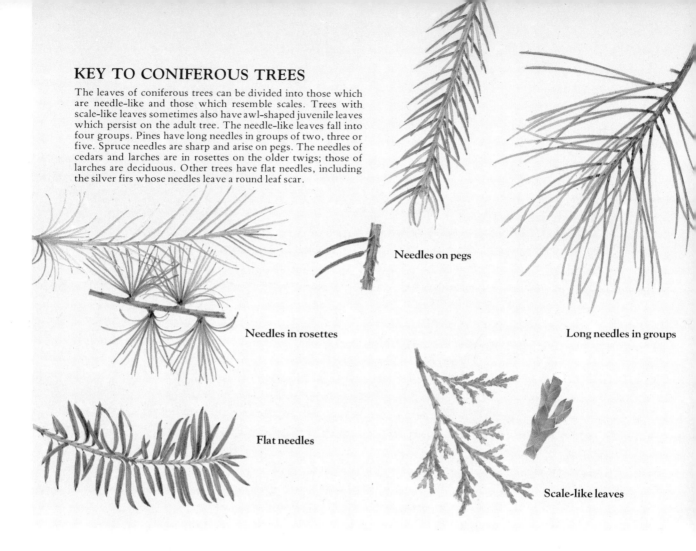

Needles on pegs

Needles in rosettes

Long needles in groups

Flat needles

Scale-like leaves

general formation. In spring and summer, the leaves and flowers are obviously the most important guides. Is the tree flowering before it has come into leaf? Are the flowers insignificant or showy? Are there two types of flowers (male and female) on the same tree or are they on separate trees? Look closely because the female flowers are often small and difficult to spot.

The leaves of deciduous trees can comprise a single blade (simple) or they can be made up of several parts (compound). How are they arranged on the twigs? What shape are they? Are the edges smooth, serrated or jagged? What size are they and what colour? When it comes to colour remember that fresh, new leaves are often quite different to the mature leaves and will probably change yet again in the autumn.

Autumn, of course, brings the main avalanche of nuts, seeds, berries and acorns, an enormous aid to positive identification. Determine whether the fruits are single or in bunches, soft, or in shells. Are the shells hard, prickly or smooth? Do the fruits sit in cups, as the acorns do, and, if so, are the cups smooth or hairy and do they sit directly on the twigs or do they have long stalks?

Once you start observing, you will notice much more than these basic points.

THE TREES

An identification guide to 84 species

●

The species are grouped according to the shape of their leaves or needles – see the explanatory key opposite, and on pages 8-9.

●

If you already know the name of a species and want to look it it up, simply consult the index.

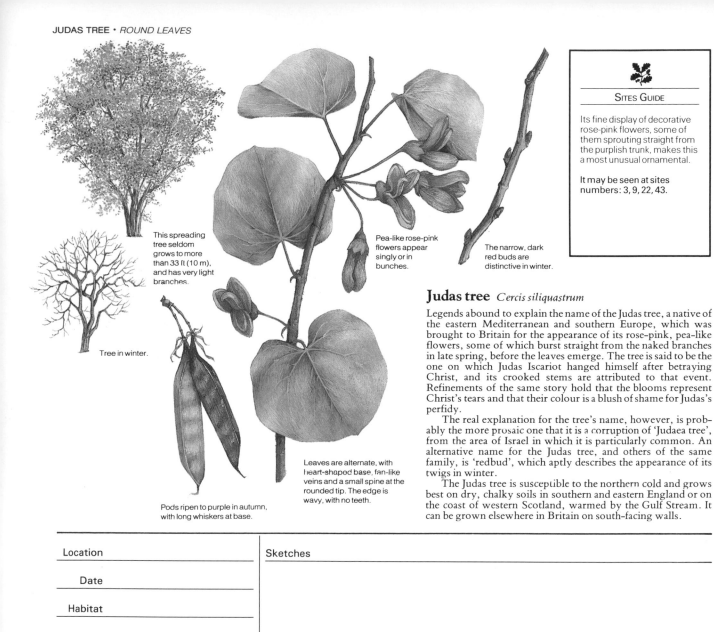

This spreading tree seldom grows to more than 33 ft (10 m), and has very light branches.

Tree in winter.

Pods ripen to purple in autumn, with long whiskers at base.

Leaves are alternate, with heart-shaped base, fan-like veins and a small spine at the rounded tip. The edge is wavy, with no teeth.

Pea-like rose-pink flowers appear singly or in bunches.

The narrow, dark red buds are distinctive in winter.

SITES GUIDE

Its fine display of decorative rose-pink flowers, some of them sprouting straight from the purplish trunk, makes this a most unusual ornamental.

It may be seen at sites numbers: 3, 9, 22, 43.

Judas tree *Cercis siliquastrum*

Legends abound to explain the name of the Judas tree, a native of the eastern Mediterranean and southern Europe, which was brought to Britain for the appearance of its rose–pink, pea-like flowers, some of which burst straight from the naked branches in late spring, before the leaves emerge. The tree is said to be the one on which Judas Iscariot hanged himself after betraying Christ, and its crooked stems are attributed to that event. Refinements of the same story hold that the blooms represent Christ's tears and that their colour is a blush of shame for Judas's perfidy.

The real explanation for the tree's name, however, is probably the more prosaic one that it is a corruption of 'Judaea tree', from the area of Israel in which it is particularly common. An alternative name for the Judas tree, and others of the same family, is 'redbud', which aptly describes the appearance of its twigs in winter.

The Judas tree is susceptible to the northern cold and grows best on dry, chalky soils in southern and eastern England or on the coast of western Scotland, warmed by the Gulf Stream. It can be grown elsewhere in Britain on south-facing walls.

Location

Date

Habitat

Sketches

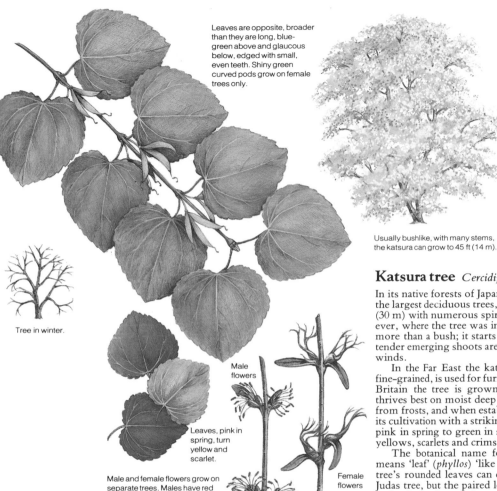

Leaves are opposite, broader than they are long, blue-green above and glaucous below, edged with small, even teeth. Shiny green curved pods grow on female trees only.

Tree in winter.

Leaves, pink in spring, turn yellow and scarlet.

Male flowers

Female flowers

Male and female flowers grow on separate trees. Males have red stamens, females have red styles.

Usually bushlike, with many stems, the katsura can grow to 45 ft (14 m).

Sites Guide

This small oriental tree is grown in the parks and gardens of Britain and Ireland for the everchanging colours of its foliage.

It may be seen at sites numbers: 3, 4, 10, 12, 15, 18, 28, 39, 43, 46, 50, 51.

Katsura tree *Cercidiphyllum japonicum*

In its native forests of Japan and China the katsura tree is one of the largest deciduous trees, reaching heights of more than 100 ft (30 m) with numerous spiral, twisting trunks. In Britain, however, where the tree was introduced in 1865, it rarely grows to more than a bush; it starts to grow early in the spring, and the tender emerging shoots are often killed by spring frosts and cold winds.

In the Far East the katsura tree's yellow timber, light and fine-grained, is used for furniture and interior woodwork, but in Britain the tree is grown for ornamental purposes only. It thrives best on moist deep soils, in parks and gardens protected from frosts, and when established it rewards the care needed for its cultivation with a striking display of leaves, which turn from pink in spring to green in summer and then to a wide range of yellows, scarlets and crimsons in autumn.

The botanical name for the katsura tree, *Cercidiphyllum*, means 'leaf' (*phyllos*) 'like the Judas tree' (*Cercis*). The katsura tree's rounded leaves can easily be confused with those of the Judas tree, but the paired leaves of the katsura tree are opposite each other, whereas those of the Judas tree are alternate.

Location

Date

Habitat

Sketches

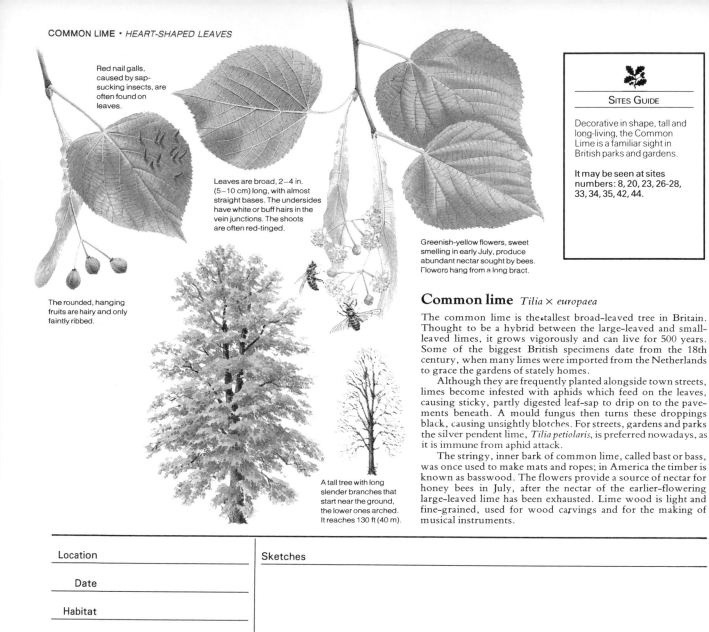

Red nail galls, caused by sap-sucking insects, are often found on leaves.

Leaves are broad, 2–4 in. (5–10 cm) long, with almost straight bases. The undersides have white or buff hairs in the vein junctions. The shoots are often red-tinged.

The rounded, hanging fruits are hairy and only faintly ribbed.

A tall tree with long slender branches that start near the ground, the lower ones arched. It reaches 130 ft (40 m).

Greenish-yellow flowers, sweet smelling in early July, produce abundant nectar sought by bees. Flowers hang from a long bract.

SITES GUIDE

Decorative in shape, tall and long-living, the Common Lime is a familiar sight in British parks and gardens.

It may be seen at sites numbers: 8, 20, 23, 26-28, 33, 34, 35, 42, 44.

Common lime *Tilia × europaea*

The common lime is the tallest broad-leaved tree in Britain. Thought to be a hybrid between the large-leaved and small-leaved limes, it grows vigorously and can live for 500 years. Some of the biggest British specimens date from the 18th century, when many limes were imported from the Netherlands to grace the gardens of stately homes.

Although they are frequently planted alongside town streets, limes become infested with aphids which feed on the leaves, causing sticky, partly digested leaf-sap to drip on to the pavements beneath. A mould fungus then turns these droppings black, causing unsightly blotches. For streets, gardens and parks the silver pendent lime, *Tilia petiolaris*, is preferred nowadays, as it is immune from aphid attack.

The stringy, inner bark of common lime, called bast or bass, was once used to make mats and ropes; in America the timber is known as basswood. The flowers provide a source of nectar for honey bees in July, after the nectar of the earlier-flowering large-leaved lime has been exhausted. Lime wood is light and fine-grained, used for wood carvings and for the making of musical instruments.

Location

Date

Habitat

Sketches

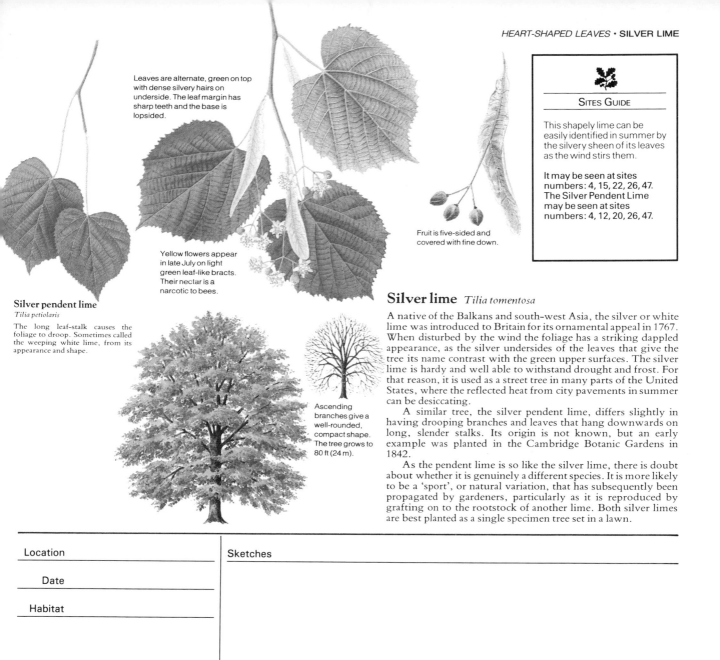

Leaves are alternate, green on top with dense silvery hairs on underside. The leaf margin has sharp teeth and the base is lopsided.

Yellow flowers appear in late July on light green leaf-like bracts. Their nectar is a narcotic to bees.

Fruit is five-sided and covered with fine down.

Silver pendent lime
Tilia petiolaris

The long leaf-stalk causes the foliage to droop. Sometimes called the weeping white lime, from its appearance and shape.

Ascending branches give a well-rounded, compact shape. The tree grows to 80 ft (24 m).

Silver lime *Tilia tomentosa*

A native of the Balkans and south-west Asia, the silver or white lime was introduced to Britain for its ornamental appeal in 1767. When disturbed by the wind the foliage has a striking dappled appearance, as the silver undersides of the leaves that give the tree its name contrast with the green upper surfaces. The silver lime is hardy and well able to withstand drought and frost. For that reason, it is used as a street tree in many parts of the United States, where the reflected heat from city pavements in summer can be desiccating.

A similar tree, the silver pendent lime, differs slightly in having drooping branches and leaves that hang downwards on long, slender stalks. Its origin is not known, but an early example was planted in the Cambridge Botanic Gardens in 1842.

As the pendent lime is so like the silver lime, there is doubt about whether it is genuinely a different species. It is more likely to be a 'sport', or natural variation, that has subsequently been propagated by gardeners, particularly as it is reproduced by grafting on to the rootstock of another lime. Both silver limes are best planted as a single specimen tree set in a lawn.

Location

Date

Habitat

Sketches

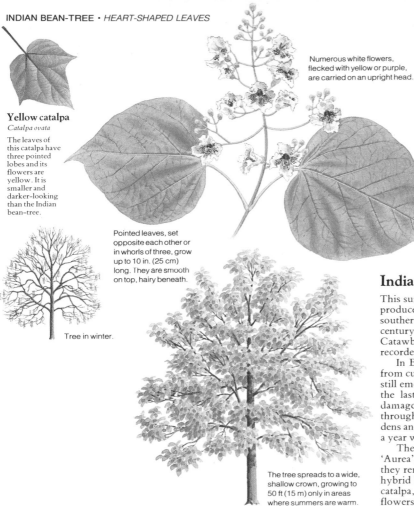

Yellow catalpa
Catalpa ovata
The leaves of this catalpa have three pointed lobes and its flowers are yellow. It is smaller and darker-looking than the Indian bean-tree.

Numerous white flowers, flecked with yellow or purple, are carried on an upright head.

Pointed leaves, set opposite each other or in whorls of three, grow up to 10 in. (25 cm) long. They are smooth on top, hairy beneath.

Tree in winter.

Bean-like pods stay on the tree all winter.

The tree spreads to a wide, shallow crown, growing to 50 ft (15 m) only in areas where summers are warm.

Indian bean-tree *Catalpa bignonioides*

This summer-flowering tree is usually the last in the garden to produce leaves: they do not appear until June. It is a native of the southern United States, first cultivated in Britain in the 18th century, and its alternative name of catalpa is a corruption of Catawba, a Red Indian tribe in the area where botanists first recorded it.

In Britain, the fruit rarely ripens and the tree is reproduced from cuttings. Because it comes into leaf so late, some leaves are still emerging when the first frost arrives, and in a hard winter the last three or four bud clusters on each branch may be damaged by the cold. Nevertheless, the catalpa flourishes throughout southern Britain where it is planted in parks, gardens and streets. It is a fast-growing tree, putting on 3–4 ft (1 m) a year when young.

The golden Indian bean-tree, a cultivated variety called 'Aurea', has deep yellow leaves if planted in the open, though they remain green if the tree is planted in shade. *Catalpa ovata*, a hybrid between the Indian bean-tree and the Chinese or yellow catalpa, has leaves that are deep purple when young. Its yellow flowers bloom in July.

Location

Date

Habitat

Sketches

The fruit is green, oval in shape and beaked. It contains winged seeds.

The leaves are opposite and felted underneath, and grow to 14 in. (36 cm) long. The stalk is hairy.

This tree has huge leaves and its flower buds are conspicuous all winter. It grows to 23 ft (7 m).

The erect, purple flowers, shaped like those of the foxglove, open in May before the leaves appear.

SITES GUIDE

One of the most striking of all ornamental trees, the Foxglove Tree is planted chiefly in the parks and gardens of southern England.

It may be seen at sites numbers: 2, 15, 21, 43.

Foxglove tree *Paulownia tomentosa*

Purple foxglove-like flowers that cover the tree in May, before the leaves appear, give this tree its common name. Young plants have been pruned back hard to produce leaves more than 24 in. (60 cm) across, giving a remarkable display of foliage. The tree's botanical name derives from Anna Paulowna (or Pavlovna), daughter of Tsar Paul I of Russia and wife of the Dutch prince who became King William II. It was named in the 17th century by the German physician and botanist Englebrecht Kaemfer, who discovered the tree on an expedition to Japan for the Dutch East India Company.

The tree came originally from China, where for hundreds of years it had been attributed with almost magical powers to preserve beauty and health. An 11th-century Chinese manuscript was devoted entirely to the tree and described, for example, how a carefully prepared infusion from its leaves and fruit would prevent the skin from wrinkling and the hair from turning grey.

The foxglove tree grows well in southern England, but its buds are vulnerable to late spring frosts. Its wood is soft when first felled, but quickly turns hard and is very light in weight.

Location	Sketches
Date	
Habitat	

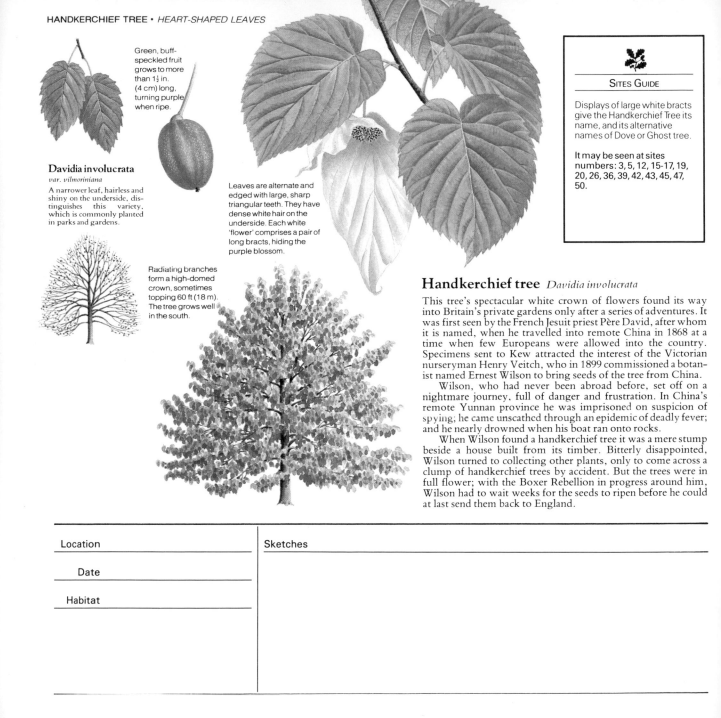

Green, buff-speckled fruit grows to more than 1½ in. (4 cm) long, turning purple when ripe.

Davidia involucrata
var. vilmoriniana

A narrower leaf, hairless and shiny on the underside, distinguishes this variety, which is commonly planted in parks and gardens.

Radiating branches form a high-domed crown, sometimes topping 60 ft (18 m). The tree grows well in the south.

Leaves are alternate and edged with large, sharp triangular teeth. They have dense white hair on the underside. Each white 'flower' comprises a pair of long bracts, hiding the purple blossom.

SITES GUIDE

Displays of large white bracts give the Handkerchief Tree its name, and its alternative names of Dove or Ghost tree.

It may be seen at sites numbers: 3, 5, 12, 15-17, 19, 20, 26, 36, 39, 42, 43, 45, 47, 50.

Handkerchief tree *Davidia involucrata*

This tree's spectacular white crown of flowers found its way into Britain's private gardens only after a series of adventures. It was first seen by the French Jesuit priest Père David, after whom it is named, when he travelled into remote China in 1868 at a time when few Europeans were allowed into the country. Specimens sent to Kew attracted the interest of the Victorian nurseryman Henry Veitch, who in 1899 commissioned a botanist named Ernest Wilson to bring seeds of the tree from China.

Wilson, who had never been abroad before, set off on a nightmare journey, full of danger and frustration. In China's remote Yunnan province he was imprisoned on suspicion of spying; he came unscathed through an epidemic of deadly fever; and he nearly drowned when his boat ran onto rocks.

When Wilson found a handkerchief tree it was a mere stump beside a house built from its timber. Bitterly disappointed, Wilson turned to collecting other plants, only to come across a clump of handkerchief trees by accident. But the trees were in full flower; with the Boxer Rebellion in progress around him, Wilson had to wait weeks for the seeds to ripen before he could at last send them back to England.

Location

Date

Habitat

Sketches

Leaves are alternate, toothed and pointed with a heart-shaped base, and hairy on both sides.

The fruit of the black mulberry is a deep wine red. It ripens in August or September.

Female flower Male flower

Sites Guide

Black Mulberries have been grown in Britain since 1550. In the north they need protection from cold winds.

They may be seen at sites numbers: 11, 16, 22, 24, 29, 33, 34, 43. White Mulberry may be seen at number 34.

In May and June, male and female flowers grow in separate catkins, sometimes on different branches.

White mulberry
Morus alba

The food plant of the silk-worm is distinguished by its shiny, less downy leaf as well as by its white or pinkish fruit.

The short trunk soon divides into spreading branches to form a bushy, round-headed tree with coarse, dark leaves, reaching 20 ft (6 m) in height.

Black mulberry *Morus nigra*

According to Classical fable, the fruit of the mulberry was once white, but was reddened by the blood of the tragic lovers Pyramus and Thisbe, whose story is parodied by Shakespeare in *A Midsummer Night's Dream*. They arranged to meet under a mulberry tree. Thisbe, who arrived first, was scared by a lion and fled, dropping her veil, which the lion smeared with blood. Pyramus, on finding it, believed Thisbe to be dead and killed himself. When Thisbe returned she committed suicide.

The fable is set in Babylon and the black, or common, mulberry may have originated in the Middle East, but it no longer grows in the wild anywhere. It was introduced to Europe by the Greeks and Romans for its fruit, which has a bitter-sweet taste and can be eaten raw or as a preserve. In the 17th century, James I encouraged the planting of black mulberry trees in an attempt to rear silk-worms for the home production of silk, but the silk-worms prefer the white mulberry, *Morus alba*, a native of China that does not grow well in Britain.

Mulberry was at one time planted in prison exercise yards. The rhyme 'Here we go round the mulberry bush' is said to have originated from daily exercise round the tree.

Location

Date

Habitat

Sketches

19

SITES GUIDE

Rocky slopes are a natural setting for the Strawberry Tree; it is sometimes planted in parks.

It may be seen at sites numbers: 15, 17, 21, 22, 33 and 39.

[× 2]

White, bell-like flowers appear in autumn, while the red strawberry-like fruits from the previous year's flowers are still ripening.

Hybrid strawberry tree
Arbutus × andrachnoides

The branches of this hybrid are red. The leaves are green on top and yellow-green beneath.

[× 2]

Leaves are alternate and evergreen, with a toothed margin. The underside is paler than the upper side, the main vein white. The stalk is short and hairy. Fruits ripen in small clusters.

This small tree, no higher than 30 ft (9 m), has twisting branches and a short trunk.

Strawberry tree *Arbutus unedo*

The popular name of this tree is derived from its round red fruits which ripen in autumn, but the fruits are not as palatable as the name suggests. In fact, the species name of *unedo* comes from the two Latin words *un edo*, 'I eat one (only)'.

The distribution of the strawberry tree is oddly patchy. In the British Isles it grows wild only in western Ireland. It occurs again in western France, and on the Mediterranean coast; but, whereas in Ireland it grows to tree size, in continental Europe it normally develops only into a shrub. One theory is that the strawberry tree has survived mainly in areas left untouched by glaciers in the Ice Age. Within historical times it certainly grew more widely than it does today, and its disappearance may well be accounted for by the fact that it makes good charcoal and burns well. Its reddish-brown wood is hard and close-grained, though liable to splitting, and is used in inlay and marquetry.

With its cinnamon-red bark the strawberry tree makes an attractive garden bush, but its seedlings need considerable protection until they are established. Though able to withstand the sea winds of the Irish coast, the tree quickly succumbs to cold northerly and easterly winds.

Location

Date

Habitat

Sketches

Cultivated apple has pinker flower.

Leaves are alternate, with pointed tips. Undersides are smooth, not hairy as on cultivated apple.

Bramley's Seedling

Cox's Orange Pippin

Numerous cultivated apples have been developed from the crab apple.

In autumn, the fruit becomes flushed with red.

The crab apple is a shrub-like tree, seldom exceeding 30 ft (9 m); its name is derived from the Norse word *skrab*, 'scrubby'.

Sites Guide

The Crab Apple is still seen in copses, thickets and hedgerows. It grows from pips dropped far and wide by people or by birds.

It may be seen at sites numbers: 11, 15, 19, 22, 27, 29, 34, 36, 38, 43, 45, 51, 55.

Crab apple *Malus sylvestris*

Small, bitter, hard and generally insignificant though its fruit may be, the humble wild crab apple is the ancestor of all the cultivated apples of today – Beauty of Bath, Laxton's Fortune and many other familiar varieties. Centuries of selection and improvement by growers have created a major food and drink industry from the cultivated apple; but the wild crab apple still has a part to play, for it continues to furnish the root stock on to which grafts are made to produce new varieties.

A wide range of ornamental flowering crab apples has been bred for street planting. In spite of its bitterness the fruit is made into jelly, jam and wine, while birds seek it out eagerly. In former times fermented crab-apple juice – called verjuice – was regarded as a remedy for scalds and sprains. The wood of crab apple, like that of cultivated apple, is excellent both for carving and for burning.

The crab apple recolonised Britain after the Ice Age and is therefore regarded as a native British tree. It is found scattered throughout the countryside, often in oak woods. The wild crab apple has thorns, which may have been intentionally bred out by growers of the cultivated apple.

Location

Date

Habitat

Sketches

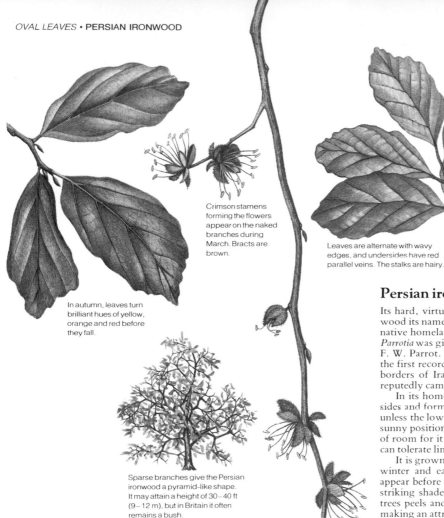

In autumn, leaves turn brilliant hues of yellow, orange and red before they fall.

Crimson stamens forming the flowers appear on the naked branches during March. Bracts are brown.

Leaves are alternate with wavy edges, and undersides have red parallel veins. The stalks are hairy.

Sparse branches give the Persian ironwood a pyramid-like shape. It may attain a height of 30–40 ft (9–12 m), but in Britain it often remains a bush.

Sites Guide

Its spectacular autumn colours have made Persian Ironwood popular for large gardens since it was first introduced in 1841.

It may be seen at sites numbers: 1, 3, 11, 12, 15, 32, 33, 39, 51.

Persian ironwood *Parrotia persica*

Its hard, virtually indestructible timber gives the Persian iron-wood its name; but the wood has no commercial use, even in its native homeland of Iran and the Caucasus. The botanical name *Parrotia* was given to this tree in honour of the Russian naturalist F. W. Parrot. Among other achievements, Parrot in 1829 made the first recorded ascent of Mount Ararat, the mountain on the borders of Iran, Turkey and Armenia on which Noah's ark reputedly came to rest.

In its homelands, the Persian ironwood grows on wet hill-sides and forms a substantial tree. In Britain, it remains a shrub unless the lower branches are pruned. It does best if planted in a sunny position on moist, well-drained soil where there is plenty of room for it to spread; unlike the closely related wych hazel it can tolerate lime.

It is grown in Britain purely for its ornamental value. In late winter and early spring it produces crimson flowers which appear before the leaves unfold, and in autumn its foliage turns striking shades of yellow, orange and red. The bark on older trees peels and flakes in patches like that of the London plane, making an attractive feature throughout the year.

Location

Date

Habitat

Sketches

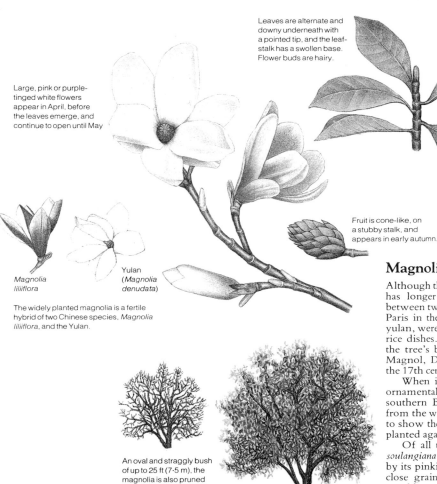

Leaves are alternate and downy underneath with a pointed tip, and the leaf-stalk has a swollen base. Flower buds are hairy.

Large, pink or purple-tinged white flowers appear in April, before the leaves emerge, and continue to open until May

Magnolia liliiflora

Yulan (*Magnolia denudata*)

The widely planted magnolia is a fertile hybrid of two Chinese species, *Magnolia liliiflora*, and the Yulan.

Fruit is cone-like, on a stubby stalk, and appears in early autumn.

SITES GUIDE

The striking pink or purple-white flowers of the popular hybrid Magnolia brighten parks and gardens in spring.

It may be seen at sites numbers: 1-6, 10, 12-16, 18-20, 24, 27, 29, 31, 32, 34, 36, 38-40, 43, 45, 46, 48-51, 55.

An oval and straggly bush of up to 25 ft (7·5 m), the magnolia is also pruned and trained against walls.

Magnolia *Magnolia × soulangiana*

Although the magnolia is a familiar feature of British gardens, it has longer associations with other countries – it is a cross between two Chinese species, and was originally cultivated near Paris in the 19th century. The buds of one of its parents, the yulan, were used by the Chinese as a medicine and for flavouring rice dishes. The French connection is continued in the use of the tree's botanical name; it commemorates Professor Pierre Magnol, Director of the Botanical Garden at Montpellier in the 17th century.

When it is in flower, the magnolia is unrivalled among ornamental shrubs. It tolerates pollution and the clay soils of southern Britain, but this deciduous shrub demands shelter from the wind and protection from spring frost if its flowers are to show their full beauty and last as long as possible. It has been planted against garden walls since Victorian times.

Of all the species of magnolia in cultivation, *Magnolia × soulangiana* is the most easily grown, and is quickly recognised by its pinkish or purplish–white flowers. The wood has a hard, close grain which has proved suitable for making angles in mouldings and on decorative woodwork.

Location	Sketches
Date	
Habitat	

The leaves are alternate and broad, with abrupt, drawn-out points and sharp teeth.

The autumn leaves, crimson or orange, fall early.

Clusters of shell-pink flowers appear in late March at the same time as the leaves.

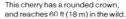

This cherry has a rounded crown, and reaches 60 ft (18 m) in the wild.

SITES GUIDE

A native of Japan and Korea, this ornamental cherry is often planted for its beautiful spring blossom.

It may be seen at sites numbers: 20, 27, 33, 45, 46.

Sargent's cherry *Prunus sargentii*

This lovely cherry is cultivated in Britain primarily for its display of pink spring blossom, but it has other ornamental features too. Its young leaves are purplish, and its autumn leaves change colour earlier than those of most trees, turning orange or crimson in September. Sargent's cherry has been widely planted in streets, gardens and parks, but unlike some other flowering cherries it has particular soil requirements, thriving best on a moist loam. However, it adapts well to the British climate, and its flower buds are not ravaged by bullfinches before they can blossom as those of other cherries are.

Charles Sprague Sargent, the American botanist after whom the cherry is named, found it in 1890, growing on mountain-sides in the shadow of Mt Fujiyama in Japan, and subsequently introduced it to the West. In Japan the even, close-grained wood is used extensively to make blocks for colour printing. It is so sought after that mature trees are now rare in their native land.

When sold by nurserymen the stem of Sargent's cherry is usually grafted on to the rootstock of its relative, the wild cherry or gean, *Prunus avium*; this produces a vigorous and attractive garden tree.

Location

Date

Habitat

Sketches

In autumn the leaf turns golden pink. Some cultivars turn red.

The large leaves have many bristly teeth and a wedge-shaped base. They have a smooth and polished appearance.

White or rose-tinged flowers appear in April or May.

The bullfinch strips cherries of their flower-buds.

This small tree with wide-spreading branches, often grafted, reaches 10–15 ft (3–4.5 m).

Sites Guide

The tree often develops a flat top. It was the first flowering cherry from the East to be planted in European gardens.

It may be seen at sites numbers: 1, 3, 6, 11, 12, 15, 18, 19, 21, 22, 24, 26, 27, 33, 34, 36, 38, 41-43, 45, 46, 55.

Japanese cherry *Prunus serrulata*

Pink and white flowers wreathing the branches of Japanese cherry trees splash many a suburban street with colour in spring. They vary widely in the precise shade of their flowers, their fragrance and the autumn and spring colours of their foliage, but they are nearly all varieties of one tree, *Prunus serrulata*.

The tree is thought to have originated in China, and then been extensively cultivated in innumerable forms in Japan. The first specimen was introduced to England via China in 1822. Most will not grow true from seed but have to be reproduced by grafting or budding, usually onto a seedling of wild cherry.

One of the most attractive Japanese cherries is 'Tai Haku', a superb, robust tree with dazzling white single flowers. For decades this tree was lost to its native land, and known to the Japanese only through paintings. It was rediscovered by Captain Collingwood Ingram, an authority on cherry trees, who in 1923 spotted a specimen growing in a garden in Sussex. Ingram realised that the tree was a rare one, and on a subsequent visit to Japan he identified it as the 'Great White Cherry' regarded by the Japanese as a long-lost species. Ingram later re-introduced the tree to its country of origin.

Location

Date

Habitat

Sketches

SITES GUIDE

Popular in Shakespeare's day for its fruit, the Medlar is now more often planted for its flowers and russet autumn leaves.

It may be seen at sites numbers: 14, 24, 31, 33, 34.

Leaves are alternate, finely toothed near the tip, hairy on the upper surface and downy beneath. A single showy flower appears at the end of each short, leafy twig in early summer, and is pollinated by bees.

The fruit, which ripens Oct. – Nov., is round and yellow-brown. A deep hollow at the end is surrounded by large, withered sepals. The fruit does not fall from the tree after ripening.

This low-growing, gnarled and rather sprawling tree grows to 20 ft (6 m).

Medlar *Mespilus germanica*

For centuries the fruit of the medlar, sometimes called 'medle' or 'merle', was a delicacy. It was eaten by the Greeks and the Romans, who dedicated it to the god Saturn, and was believed by herbalists to cure a variety of ailments, including excessive bleeding, kidney stones and digestive disorders.

Medlar fruit cannot be eaten raw until it is 'bletted' – that is, allowed to become over-ripe to the point at which the flesh softens and starts to rot, but before the outer skin shows signs of decay. If the fruit is left on the tree, frost will start the bletting process. Alternatively, the medlars can be picked in the autumn and laid out under cover for two weeks or so to soften. The need to let medlars blet was well known to Shakespeare, who punned on the fruit's name in *As You Like It* Rosalind tells the interfering clown Touchstone: 'You'll be rotten ere you be half-ripe, and that's the right virtue of the medlar.'

Medlar fruit can also be made into jelly, but the tree is now more commonly grown for ornament. An infertile form called Smith's medlar, which flowers profusely, is a cross between the medlar and the hawthorn. Medlars originally came from the Caucasus, and some now grow wild in south-east England.

Location		Sketches
Date		
Habitat		

Leaves are alternate, similar to those of holm oak, but they have spine-tipped lobes. They are dark green on top, white underneath. Acorns are in a loose, shallow cup.

The evergreen cork oak, native to the Mediterranean, has low gnarled branches. It grows to 65 ft (20 m).

Female flowers appear on the young, grey-green shoots in May or June.

SITES GUIDE

In Portugal and Spain these trees are stripped for their cork, revealing the red inner bark. In Britain the trees are only ornamental.

They may be seen at sites numbers: 3-5, 13, 17, 26, 28, 34, 40, 46.

Cork oak *Quercus suber*

Every ten years or so the cork oaks of Portugal, Spain and Algeria have the outer bark stripped from their trunks to furnish the world with bottle stoppers, insulating materials, flooring tiles and other cork products. In Britain cork oaks are not exploited commercially, but grown simply for their ornamental value as attractive evergreens.

Cork is light, buoyant and impervious to liquids, and it does not conduct heat. These qualities have been known to man for 2,000 years: the Romans used cork to make sandals and floats to buoy up fishing nets. But it was not until glass bottles were first manufactured on a large scale in the 15th to 16th centuries that the foundations of the modern cork industry were laid.

In Mediterranean lands, the cork is cut from the tree in rings up to 3 in. (7·5 cm) thick, using an axe. The tree then survives to grow another layer; some 500-year-old Portuguese oaks have been stripped 40 or 50 times. Care has to be taken not to damage the living tissue immediately below the bark, for this layer transports the food manufactured in the leaves to all parts of the tree. In Britain animals such as ponies and squirrels can kill some types of tree by eating the bark right round the trunk.

Location	Sketches
Date	
Habitat	

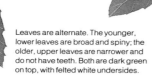

Leaves are alternate. The younger, lower leaves are broad and spiny; the older, upper leaves are narrower and do not have teeth. Both are dark green on top, with felted white undersides.

Light green acorns are up to two-thirds enclosed in their scaly cups. [Actual size]

Male flowers are long yellow catkins, appearing in June.

SITES GUIDE

Salt-laden sea winds do not harm the rugged Holm Oak, which flourishes even in exposed sites on coasts and estuaries.

It may be seen at sites numbers: 1, 4, 12, 16, 23, 26, 28, 33, 34, 46, 47.

The evergreen holm oak grows into a round-headed tree up to 90 ft (27 m) high.

Holm oak *Quercus ilex*

Most kinds of oak familiar in Britain lose their leaves in winter, but holm oak is one of the evergreen species. Its leaves are spiky when young and give the tree its names in English and Latin: holm and *ilex*, both mean holly. In some parts of England the tree is called the holly oak or the live oak, as it remains 'alive', or green, through the winter.

Holm oak is native to the Mediterranean lands and was brought to Britain more than 400 years ago. It is very hardy and grows well on most poor soils, although it does not like heavy clay. Its leaves are adapted to withstand drying out in hot dry summers, so it flourishes in exposed locations, particularly by the sea, where it is useful for shade or, if clipped back hard, for hedging.

In southern Europe the hard, dense wood is used in furniture making and for the handles of tools, and also as a source of charcoal. As with other oaks, the freshly cut timber produces a blue stain around nails driven into it, as the tannin in the wood reacts with the iron. The presence of tannin made the holm oak a source of material for treating leather and skins in Greek and Roman times.

Location	Sketches
Date	
Habitat	

SITES GUIDE

A dainty native of the Far East, the Snowbell Tree needs little room to grow and is suitable for planting in small gardens.

It may be seen at sites numbers: 12, 13, 15, 18, 19, 27, 41, 43.

Greenish egg-shaped fruits hang down on long stalks, splitting in autumn to show brown seeds.

Leaves are alternate and taper at both ends, with a few very small teeth on the edges. The snowdrop-like flowers, with yellow stamens, bloom in mid-June.

Tree in winter.

The snowbell tree is broader than it is tall. It can grow to 30 ft (9 m).

Snowbell tree *Styrax japonica*

Masses of snowy-white, delicate flowers which hang under the fan-like branches in early summer give the snowbell tree its common English name. It was brought from Japan at the end of the last century purely as an ornamental tree, but in the Far East its light, yellowish, soft and close-grained timber is used for household utensils and decorative carving.

The snowbell flowers can be best appreciated if they are seen from below, so the tree should be planted on rising ground or a grassy knoll. The snowbell thrives in sunny places on rich, lime-free soils and is quite hardy, though it may be damaged if the tissues of its twigs and buds thaw out too quickly after frost in early spring.

Other types of snowbell tree are also grown in British gardens, including one from the Mediterranean which is the source of a balsam or aromatic gum called storax. This is obtained by making incisions in the bark and then collecting the liquid that exudes from it. Balsam was formerly used in medicine to treat asthma and bronchitis, and is still burned as incense. In some European countries, hardened drops of balsam are made into rosary beads.

Location	Sketches
Date	
Habitat	

29

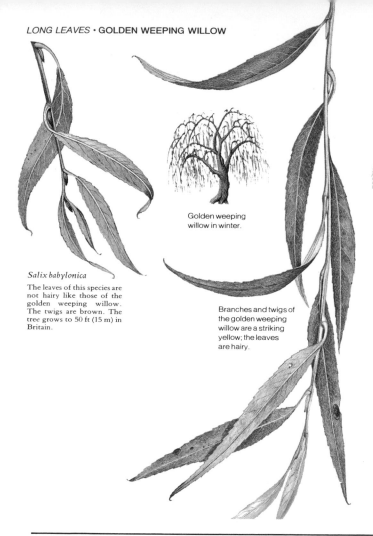

Golden weeping
willow in winter.

Salix babylonica
The leaves of this species are
not hairy like those of the
golden weeping willow.
The twigs are brown. The
tree grows to 50 ft (15 m) in
Britain.

Branches and twigs of
the golden weeping
willow are a striking
yellow; the leaves
are hairy.

From its early days, the golden
weeping willow produces a round
cascade of yellow twigs and green
leaves, reaching almost to the
ground. It grows to 65 ft (20 m).

Golden weeping willow *Salix × chrysocoma* (or 'Tristis')

Small, creeping willows were among the earliest trees to
recolonise Britain after the Ice Age. Since then, so many species
have evolved that it is very difficult to tell them apart. Most
willows hybridise freely with one another. Of the weeping
willows planted in the past, many were selections and crosses
propagated by nurseries, and have been given different names
according to different opinions about their origins.

The most commonly planted ornamental weeping willow
today is golden weeping willow, thought to be a cross between
Salix babylonica and a form of *Salix alba*. Golden weeping willow
is a fast-growing tree that can be propagated by pushing a long
twig into the ground; it will soon root itself and grow into a
graceful sapling.

Weeping willows have traditionally been regarded as sym-
bols of mourning. The botanical name *Salix babylonica* recalls the
sadness of the Psalm: 'By the rivers of Babylon, there we sat
down, yea, we wept. . . . Upon the willows in the midst thereof
we hanged up our harps.' In fact the riverside trees of Babylon
were poplars, not willows; the species of willow known as
babylonica is now known to have originated in China.

Location	Sketches
Date	
Habitat	

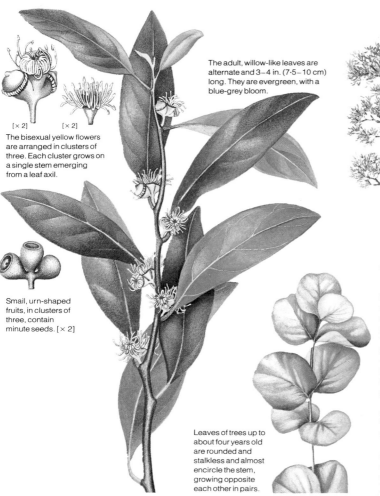

[× 2]   [× 2]

The bisexual yellow flowers are arranged in clusters of three. Each cluster grows on a single stem emerging from a leaf axil.

The adult, willow-like leaves are alternate and 3–4 in. (7·5–10 cm) long. They are evergreen, with a blue-grey bloom.

Small, urn-shaped fruits, in clusters of three, contain minute seeds. [× 2]

Leaves of trees up to about four years old are rounded and stalkless and almost encircle the stem, growing opposite each other in pairs.

A tall, graceful and very open tree that grows up to 100 ft (30 m).

Sites Guide

This fast-growing eucalyptus, sometimes known as Tasmanian Cider Gum, is popular as an ornamental garden tree.

It may be seen at sites numbers: 1, 12, 14, 38, 43, 46, 51-53.

Cider gum *Eucalyptus gunnii*

Several species of gum tree, or eucalyptus, have been introduced into Britain from Australasia for their ornamental qualities. The cider gum, which comes from the cool mountain regions of southern Australia and Tasmania, is the most widespread in gardens and parks. Its round juvenile leaves, which it puts forth until it is about four years old, are widely used in flower arrangements. Cider gums thrive on most soils, apart from chalk, as far north as Scotland. In common with other gums, they do not form winter buds but continue growing; as a result their younger leaves are susceptible to frost. If a frost–damaged gum is cut down to ground level it will reshoot from the base.

Compared with some forest giants in the gum family the cider gum is small, reaching a maximum height of 100 ft (30 m). The giant *Eucalyptus regnans*, for instance, grows to more than three times that height.

Gum trees take their name from the resinous substance that they exude from their bark. The leaves of many species give off the distinctive smell of eucalyptus oil when crushed, but those of the cider gum are practically odourless. The flowers have a hinged lid that opens to allow insects to pollinate them.

Location

Date

Habitat

Sketches

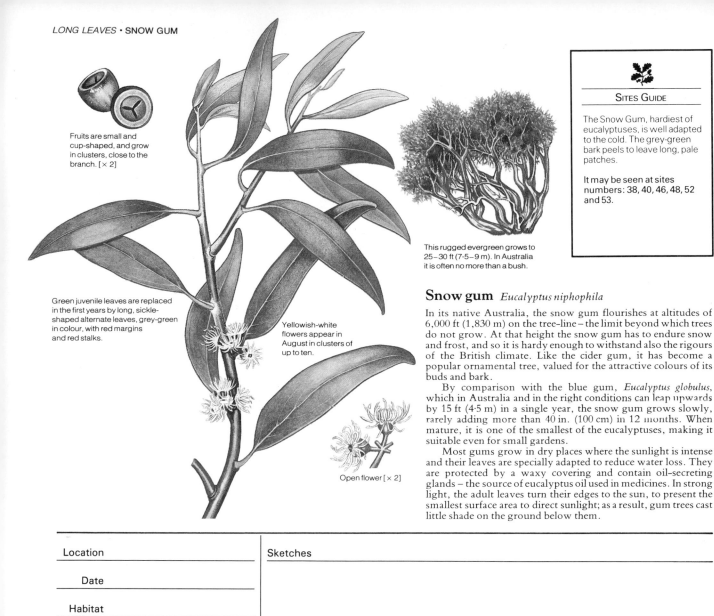

Fruits are small and cup-shaped, and grow in clusters, close to the branch. [× 2]

Green juvenile leaves are replaced in the first years by long, sickle-shaped alternate leaves, grey-green in colour, with red margins and red stalks.

Yellowish-white flowers appear in August in clusters of up to ten.

Open flower [× 2]

This rugged evergreen grows to 25–30 ft (7·5–9 m). In Australia it is often no more than a bush.

Snow gum *Eucalyptus niphophila*

In its native Australia, the snow gum flourishes at altitudes of 6,000 ft (1,830 m) on the tree-line – the limit beyond which trees do not grow. At that height the snow gum has to endure snow and frost, and so it is hardy enough to withstand also the rigours of the British climate. Like the cider gum, it has become a popular ornamental tree, valued for the attractive colours of its buds and bark.

By comparison with the blue gum, *Eucalyptus globulus*, which in Australia and in the right conditions can leap upwards by 15 ft (4·5 m) in a single year, the snow gum grows slowly, rarely adding more than 40 in. (100 cm) in 12 months. When mature, it is one of the smallest of the eucalyptuses, making it suitable even for small gardens.

Most gums grow in dry places where the sunlight is intense and their leaves are specially adapted to reduce water loss. They are protected by a waxy covering and contain oil-secreting glands – the source of eucalyptus oil used in medicines. In strong light, the adult leaves turn their edges to the sun, to present the smallest surface area to direct sunlight; as a result, gum trees cast little shade on the ground below them.

Location

Date

Habitat

Sketches

SITES GUIDE

This tree from the Caucasus is planted in large gardens for the sake of its butter-yellow autumn foliage.

It may be seen at sites numbers: 6, 26, 31, 36, 42, 52, 55.

The paired seeds are in clusters of 'keys'. Each pair has widely spread wings about 1½ in. (4 cm) long.

Leaves are opposite with five to seven untoothed, long-pointed, triangular lobes. They are smooth except for tufts of hair in vein axils on the underside.

The pale yellow flowers open in sprays in May as the leaves emerge.

Cappadocian maple has a broad, rounded, shapely outline with dense foliage. It has a short trunk and twisting branches, and can reach a height of 80 ft (24 m).

Cappadocian maple *Acer cappadocicum*

Most maples become a delight to the eye in their autumn colours, but two park and garden cultivars of the Cappadocian maple provide a splash of colour in spring as well. The leaves of the cultivar 'Aureum' are pale yellow as they unfold in spring, turning to green in summer and a rich butter-yellow in autumn.

The leaves of another cultivar, 'Rubrum', are red when they first come out, then turn a golden yellow. Later in the summer these leaves fade to green, but in some trees there is further growth, which is yellow. The paler parts of these leaves lack some of the pigments which constitute chlorophyll, the chemical that normally gives leaves their green colour and absorbs energy from sunlight to power the food-manufacturing processes of trees and plants.

The Cappadocian maple is a native of the Caucasus, the Himalayas and China. It derives its name from an ancient region of Asia Minor which is the mountainous central area of present-day Turkey. The tree was introduced to Britain 100 years ago. It is hardy and fast-growing and does well in most soils. It never attains a great height, and is therefore being increasingly planted for ornament in large gardens.

Location	Sketches
Date	
Habitat	

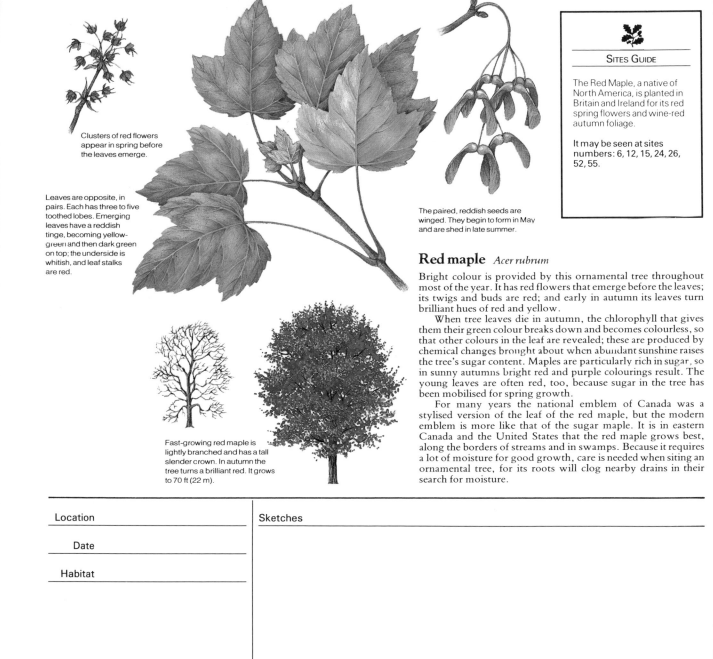

Clusters of red flowers appear in spring before the leaves emerge.

Leaves are opposite, in pairs. Each has three to five toothed lobes. Emerging leaves have a reddish tinge, becoming yellow-green and then dark green on top; the underside is whitish, and leaf stalks are red.

The paired, reddish seeds are winged. They begin to form in May and are shed in late summer.

Fast-growing red maple is lightly branched and has a tall slender crown. In autumn the tree turns a brilliant red. It grows to 70 ft (22 m).

SITES GUIDE

The Red Maple, a native of North America, is planted in Britain and Ireland for its red spring flowers and wine-red autumn foliage.

It may be seen at sites numbers: 6, 12, 15, 24, 26, 52, 55.

Red maple *Acer rubrum*

Bright colour is provided by this ornamental tree throughout most of the year. It has red flowers that emerge before the leaves; its twigs and buds are red; and early in autumn its leaves turn brilliant hues of red and yellow.

When tree leaves die in autumn, the chlorophyll that gives them their green colour breaks down and becomes colourless, so that other colours in the leaf are revealed; these are produced by chemical changes brought about when abundant sunshine raises the tree's sugar content. Maples are particularly rich in sugar, so in sunny autumns bright red and purple colourings result. The young leaves are often red, too, because sugar in the tree has been mobilised for spring growth.

For many years the national emblem of Canada was a stylised version of the leaf of the red maple, but the modern emblem is more like that of the sugar maple. It is in eastern Canada and the United States that the red maple grows best, along the borders of streams and in swamps. Because it requires a lot of moisture for good growth, care is needed when siting an ornamental tree, for its roots will clog nearby drains in their search for moisture.

Location

Date

Habitat

Sketches

Greenish-red or dark red flowers appear on the shoots in March, before the leaves.

SITES GUIDE

The handsome Silver Maple, from eastern North America, is often planted in parks and beside main roads.

It may be seen at sites numbers: 2, 3, 12, 26, 28, 31, 34, 47, 52, 55.

Slender branches of the silver maple thrust strongly upward, spreading near the top, to give the tree a tall, open appearance. It grows to about 100 ft (30 m).

Tree in winter.

Leaves are opposite, in pairs, and have five deeply divided lobes with large, irregular teeth. Undersides are silvery.

Paired seeds are set close together and have twisted wings.

In autumn, leaves turn a delicate yellow, and sometimes a brilliant red.

Silver maple *Acer saccharinum*

Like most members of the maple family, the silver maple has sap so rich in sugar that in its North American homeland it is exploited commercially to produce both syrup and refined sugar. The tree can be tapped every year so long as it is healthy and growing in favourable conditions, such as the deep, wet soils of swamps and by riversides.

Incisions are made in the bark in February and collecting tubes are inserted. The sap is taken out daily for about six weeks. After that, the concentration of sugar in it falls, and collecting it becomes uneconomical. The collected sap is concentrated by boiling it into maple syrup; it is then sold in this form or refined into sugar. As it contains certain aromatic substances, the syrup and sugar have a distinctive flavour. The silver maple was the chief source of sugar for the early settlers of North America.

In Britain the tree yields little sugar, but it flourishes as an ornamental tree when planted on suitable sites. It is hardy and only casts a light shade. One disadvantage is that the twigs are rather brittle and easily snapped by the wind. But in light winds the tree is seen to advantage, as the undersides of the leaves reveal their silvery colour.

Location

Date

Habitat

Sketches

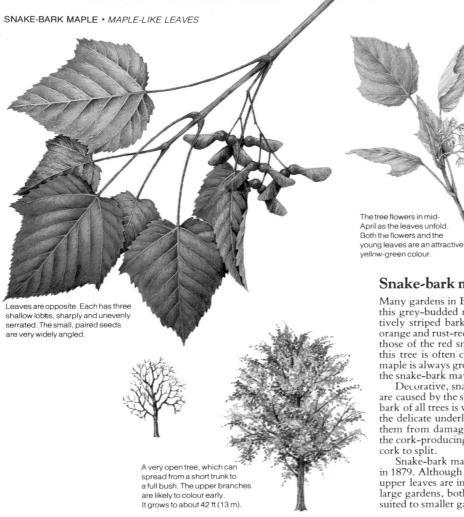

Leaves are opposite. Each has three shallow lobes, sharply and unevenly serrated. The small, paired seeds are very widely angled.

The tree flowers in mid-April as the leaves unfold. Both the flowers and the young leaves are an attractive yellow-green colour.

A very open tree, which can spread from a short trunk to a full bush. The upper branches are likely to colour early. It grows to about 42 ft (13 m).

Sites Guide

This often short-lived tree flowers abundantly from an early age. Its bark is green and white or grey and pink.

It may be seen at sites numbers: 3, 6, 10, 13, 15, 27, 34, 42, 45, 52, 55.

Snake-bark maple *Acer rufinerve*

Many gardens in Britain and Japan owe some of their beauty to this grey-budded maple, which is grown mainly for its attractively striped bark. In autumn, the leaves add their splash of orange and rust-red colour to the scene. The leaves are similar to those of the red snake-bark maple, *Acer capillipes*, with which this tree is often confused; but the bark of the red snake-bark maple is always green with white or buff stripes, whereas that of the snake-bark may be either green and white or grey and pink.

Decorative, snakeskin-like patterns on the bark of older trees are caused by the splitting of the bark's outer layer of cork. The bark of all trees is waterproof and contains cork which prevents the delicate underlying tissues from drying out, and also saves them from damage by animals and insects. As the tree grows, the cork-producing cells expand, causing the dead outer layer of cork to split.

Snake-bark maple was brought to Britain from the Far East in 1879. Although it is hardy and can be grown in most soils, its upper leaves are inclined to colour early. It is mainly grown in large gardens, both in Britain and in Japan; but in fact it is also suited to smaller gardens, as it does not reach a great height.

Location	Sketches
Date	
Habitat	

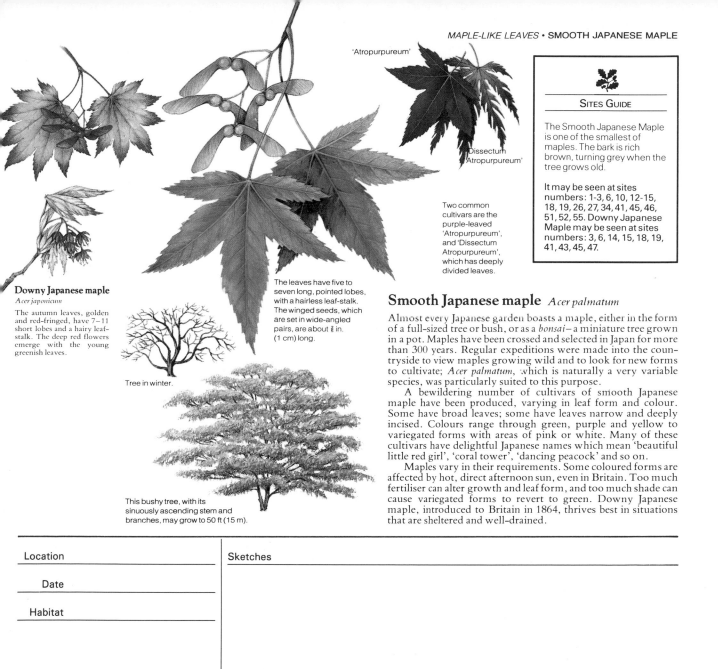

'Atropurpureum'

Dissectum
'Atropurpureum'

Two common
cultivars are the
purple-leaved
'Atropurpureum',
and 'Dissectum
Atropurpureum',
which has deeply
divided leaves.

Downy Japanese maple
Acer japonicum

The autumn leaves, golden
and red-fringed, have 7–11
short lobes and a hairy leaf-
stalk. The deep red flowers
emerge with the young
greenish leaves.

Tree in winter.

The leaves have five to
seven long, pointed lobes,
with a hairless leaf-stalk.
The winged seeds, which
are set in wide-angled
pairs, are about ⅖ in.
(1 cm) long.

This bushy tree, with its
sinuously ascending stem and
branches, may grow to 50 ft (15 m).

Sites Guide

The Smooth Japanese Maple
is one of the smallest of
maples. The bark is rich
brown, turning grey when the
tree grows old.

It may be seen at sites
numbers: 1-3, 6, 10, 12-15,
18, 19, 26, 27, 34, 41, 45, 46,
51, 52, 55. Downy Japanese
Maple may be seen at sites
numbers: 3, 6, 14, 15, 18, 19,
41, 43, 45, 47.

Smooth Japanese maple *Acer palmatum*

Almost every Japanese garden boasts a maple, either in the form
of a full-sized tree or bush, or as a *bonsai*—a miniature tree grown
in a pot. Maples have been crossed and selected in Japan for more
than 300 years. Regular expeditions were made into the countryside to view maples growing wild and to look for new forms
to cultivate; *Acer palmatum*, which is naturally a very variable
species, was particularly suited to this purpose.

A bewildering number of cultivars of smooth Japanese
maple have been produced, varying in leaf form and colour.
Some have broad leaves; some have leaves narrow and deeply
incised. Colours range through green, purple and yellow to
variegated forms with areas of pink or white. Many of these
cultivars have delightful Japanese names which mean 'beautiful
little red girl', 'coral tower', 'dancing peacock' and so on.

Maples vary in their requirements. Some coloured forms are
affected by hot, direct afternoon sun, even in Britain. Too much
fertiliser can alter growth and leaf form, and too much shade can
cause variegated forms to revert to green. Downy Japanese
maple, introduced to Britain in 1864, thrives best in situations
that are sheltered and well-drained.

Location

Date

Habitat

Sketches

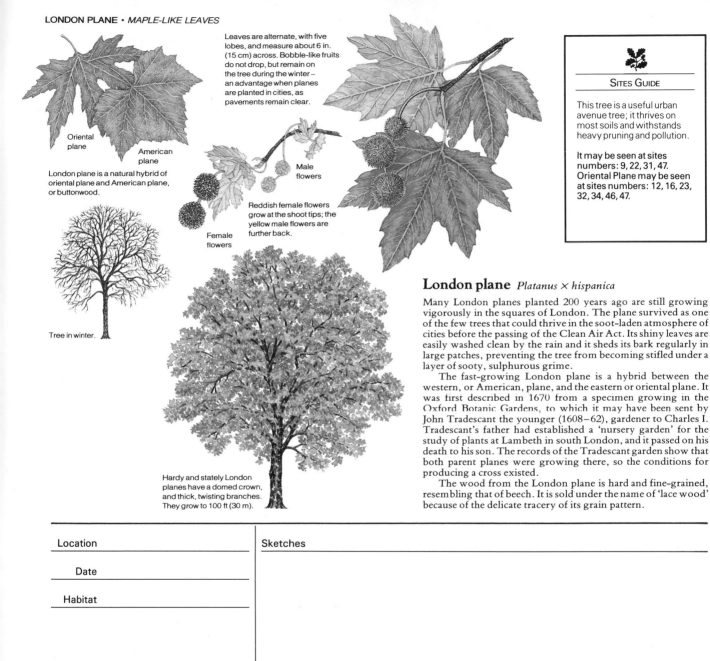

Leaves are alternate, with five lobes, and measure about 6 in. (15 cm) across. Bobble-like fruits do not drop, but remain on the tree during the winter – an advantage when planes are planted in cities, as pavements remain clear.

Oriental plane

American plane

London plane is a natural hybrid of oriental plane and American plane, or buttonwood.

Male flowers

Reddish female flowers grow at the shoot tips; the yellow male flowers are further back.

Female flowers

Tree in winter.

Hardy and stately London planes have a domed crown, and thick, twisting branches. They grow to 100 ft (30 m).

SITES GUIDE

This tree is a useful urban avenue tree; it thrives on most soils and withstands heavy pruning and pollution.

It may be seen at sites numbers: 9, 22, 31, 47. Oriental Plane may be seen at sites numbers: 12, 16, 23, 32, 34, 46, 47.

London plane *Platanus × hispanica*

Many London planes planted 200 years ago are still growing vigorously in the squares of London. The plane survived as one of the few trees that could thrive in the soot-laden atmosphere of cities before the passing of the Clean Air Act. Its shiny leaves are easily washed clean by the rain and it sheds its bark regularly in large patches, preventing the tree from becoming stifled under a layer of sooty, sulphurous grime.

The fast-growing London plane is a hybrid between the western, or American, plane, and the eastern or oriental plane. It was first described in 1670 from a specimen growing in the Oxford Botanic Gardens, to which it may have been sent by John Tradescant the younger (1608–62), gardener to Charles I. Tradescant's father had established a 'nursery garden' for the study of plants at Lambeth in south London, and it passed on his death to his son. The records of the Tradescant garden show that both parent planes were growing there, so the conditions for producing a cross existed.

The wood from the London plane is hard and fine-grained, resembling that of beech. It is sold under the name of 'lace wood' because of the delicate tracery of its grain pattern.

Location

Date

Habitat

Sketches

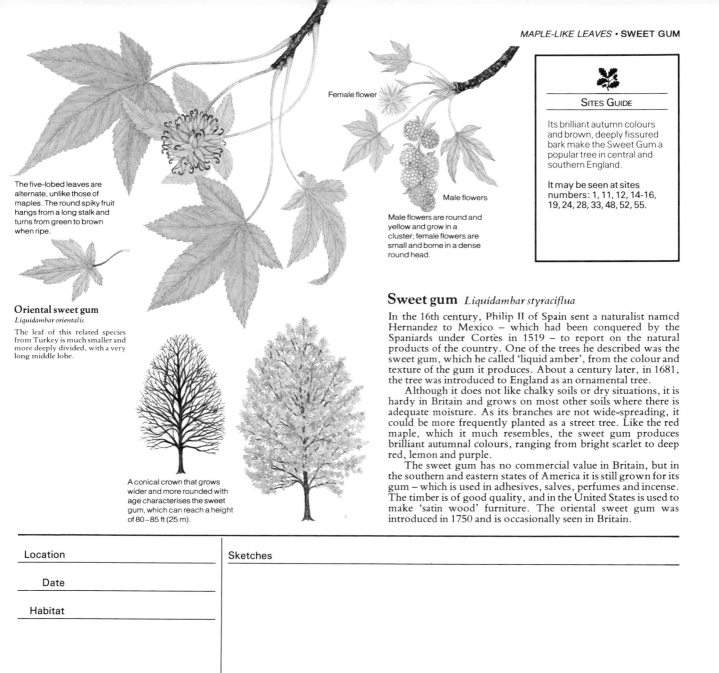

Female flower

The five-lobed leaves are alternate, unlike those of maples. The round spiky fruit hangs from a long stalk and turns from green to brown when ripe.

Male flowers

Male flowers are round and yellow and grow in a cluster; female flowers are small and borne in a dense round head.

Oriental sweet gum
Liquidambar orientalis

The leaf of this related species from Turkey is much smaller and more deeply divided, with a very long middle lobe.

A conical crown that grows wider and more rounded with age characterises the sweet gum, which can reach a height of 80–85 ft (25 m).

Sites Guide

Its brilliant autumn colours and brown, deeply fissured bark make the Sweet Gum a popular tree in central and southern England.

It may be seen at sites numbers: 1, 11, 12, 14-16, 19, 24, 28, 33, 48, 52, 55.

Sweet gum *Liquidambar styraciflua*

In the 16th century, Philip II of Spain sent a naturalist named Hernandez to Mexico – which had been conquered by the Spaniards under Cortès in 1519 – to report on the natural products of the country. One of the trees he described was the sweet gum, which he called 'liquid amber', from the colour and texture of the gum it produces. About a century later, in 1681, the tree was introduced to England as an ornamental tree.

Although it does not like chalky soils or dry situations, it is hardy in Britain and grows on most other soils where there is adequate moisture. As its branches are not wide-spreading, it could be more frequently planted as a street tree. Like the red maple, which it much resembles, the sweet gum produces brilliant autumnal colours, ranging from bright scarlet to deep red, lemon and purple.

The sweet gum has no commercial value in Britain, but in the southern and eastern states of America it is still grown for its gum – which is used in adhesives, salves, perfumes and incense. The timber is of good quality, and in the United States is used to make 'satin wood' furniture. The oriental sweet gum was introduced in 1750 and is occasionally seen in Britain.

Location

Date

Habitat

Sketches

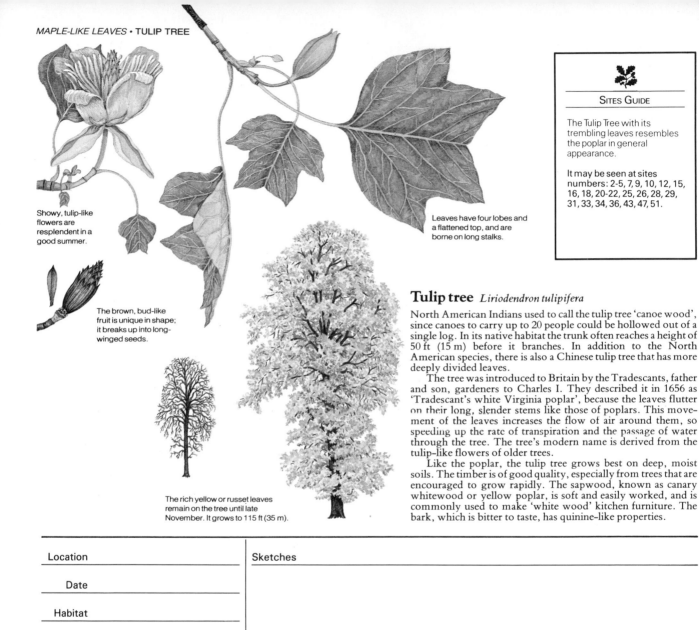

Showy, tulip-like flowers are resplendent in a good summer.

The brown, bud-like fruit is unique in shape; it breaks up into long-winged seeds.

Leaves have four lobes and a flattened top, and are borne on long stalks.

The rich yellow or russet leaves remain on the tree until late November. It grows to 115 ft (35 m).

SITES GUIDE

The Tulip Tree with its trembling leaves resembles the poplar in general appearance.

It may be seen at sites numbers: 2-5, 7, 9, 10, 12, 15, 16, 18, 20-22, 25, 26, 28, 29, 31, 33, 34, 36, 43, 47, 51.

Tulip tree *Liriodendron tulipifera*

North American Indians used to call the tulip tree 'canoe wood', since canoes to carry up to 20 people could be hollowed out of a single log. In its native habitat the trunk often reaches a height of 50 ft (15 m) before it branches. In addition to the North American species, there is also a Chinese tulip tree that has more deeply divided leaves.

The tree was introduced to Britain by the Tradescants, father and son, gardeners to Charles I. They described it in 1656 as 'Tradescant's white Virginia poplar', because the leaves flutter on their long, slender stems like those of poplars. This movement of the leaves increases the flow of air around them, so speeding up the rate of transpiration and the passage of water through the tree. The tree's modern name is derived from the tulip-like flowers of older trees.

Like the poplar, the tulip tree grows best on deep, moist soils. The timber is of good quality, especially from trees that are encouraged to grow rapidly. The sapwood, known as canary whitewood or yellow poplar, is soft and easily worked, and is commonly used to make 'white wood' kitchen furniture. The bark, which is bitter to taste, has quinine-like properties.

Location	Sketches
Date	
Habitat	

First-year acorns.

The leaf turns a dark red in autumn.

Acorns are held in shallow, saucer-like cups; they ripen in their second year.

Tree in winter.

Leaves are alternate, broader than those of scarlet oak, with shorter, stouter stalks. Both sides are matt green.

This North American oak has a large dome with straight branches. It reaches 115 ft (35 m).

Sites Guide

The Red Oak is fast-growing. Although it is common in parks and gardens, it is also often used to screen conifer plantations.

It may be seen at sites numbers: 3, 10, 12, 15, 18, 25-28, 30, 31, 33, 47.

Red oak *Quercus borealis*

In its choice of habitat the red oak falls between scarlet oak and pin oak, growing best on deep, well-drained soil, where it grows rapidly into a big tree. The red oak does not tolerate a lot of shade, so it prefers open situations in which it can spread itself without competition. Like the other red oaks, *Quercus borealis* (the red oak proper) is planted for its autumn colour, which in this species colours the entire crown at the same time.

Red oaks in America are susceptible to a disease known as oak wilt, caused by a fungus of the same type that attacks elm trees and carried in a similar way by bark beetles. The onset of oak wilt is signalled by a browning of the leaves. Stringent precautions are being taken to prevent the disease from entering Britain; when red oak timber is imported, the beetles are killed before shipment by de-barking and fumigation.

The Forestry Commission has planted red oaks on the edge of woodland rides to add diversity and colour to commercial plantations. The tree has not, however, proved a success as a city tree: the crowns are too broad for avenues, and the fallen leaves make pavements slippery in the autumn. In its native America the tannin-rich bark was used for tanning leather.

Location

Date

Habitat

Sketches

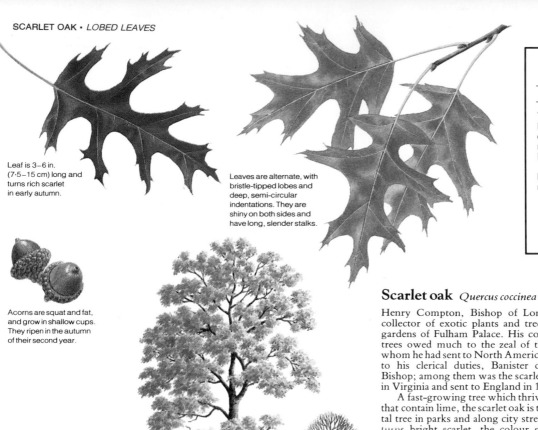

Leaf is 3–6 in. (7·5–15 cm) long and turns rich scarlet in early autumn.

Leaves are alternate, with bristle-tipped lobes and deep, semi-circular indentations. They are shiny on both sides and have long, slender stalks.

Acorns are squat and fat, and grow in shallow cups. They ripen in the autumn of their second year.

A tall-domed tree with a slender trunk and many fine upswept branches in the crown. It reaches 85 ft (26 m).

Sites Guide

This oak provides some of Britain's richest autumn colour. It is often planted on roadsides, mainly in southern England.

It may be seen at sites numbers: 14, 15, 26, 43.

Scarlet oak *Quercus coccinea*

Henry Compton, Bishop of London in 1675, was an avid collector of exotic plants and trees with which he filled the gardens of Fulham Palace. His collection of North American trees owed much to the zeal of the Reverend John Banister, whom he had sent to North America as a missionary. In addition to his clerical duties, Banister collected specimens for the Bishop; among them was the scarlet oak, which Banister found in Virginia and sent to England in 1691.

A fast-growing tree which thrives on most soils except those that contain lime, the scarlet oak is today planted as an ornamental tree in parks and along city streets. In a dry autumn the tree turns bright scarlet, the colour spreading like a blush from branch to branch instead of appearing suddenly throughout the crown as in most other trees. Scarlet oak in its native home cannot tolerate shade, and is not found in dense woodland; it is usually scattered wherever there is adequate light.

The wood of the scarlet oak is heavy, hard and strong. But unlike that of the white oaks that are native to Britain, the timber of the scarlet oak is not resistant to decay. It is, however, imported for making whisky barrels in Scotland.

Location

Date

Habitat

Sketches

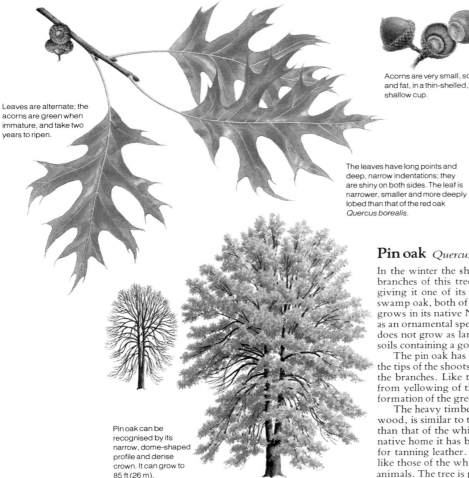

Leaves are alternate; the acorns are green when immature, and take two years to ripen.

Acorns are very small, squat and fat, in a thin-shelled, shallow cup.

The leaves have long points and deep, narrow indentations; they are shiny on both sides. The leaf is narrower, smaller and more deeply lobed than that of the red oak *Quercus borealis.*

Pin oak can be recognised by its narrow, dome-shaped profile and dense crown. It can grow to 85 ft (26 m).

Pin oak *Quercus palustris*

In the winter the short, slender twigs that stand out from the branches of this tree have a pin-like appearance at a distance, giving it one of its names. It is also known as water oak and swamp oak, both of which names describe situations in which it grows in its native North America. In Britain the tree is grown as an ornamental species, on a wide variety of soils. Although it does not grow as large as the red oak, it probably does best on soils containing a good deal of moisture.

The pin oak has brilliant red autumn colouring that starts at the tips of the shoots before spreading to the rest of the leaves on the branches. Like the other red oaks, it grows fast but suffers from yellowing of the leaves on chalky soils, which inhibit the formation of the green pigment chlorophyll.

The heavy timber of the pin oak, with its red-brown heart-wood, is similar to that of other red oaks, and of poorer quality than that of the white oaks, being less resistant to decay. In its native home it has been used for making charcoal, and its bark for tanning leather. The acorn is bitter with tannin, not sweet like those of the white oaks, and is not so attractive to foraging animals. The tree is planted mainly in southern England.

Location	Sketches
Date	
Habitat	

The acorn cup has large, loose-fitting scales.

Leaves are alternate, about 8 in. (20 cm) long with many deep lobes. They taper towards the stalk and are dark green above, grey and hairy below.

Tree in winter.

Branches fan out to a large domed crown. The tree reaches 90 ft (27 m).

Hungarian oak *Quercus frainetto*

This stately, ornamental oak has not been widely planted in Britain, and most of the specimens found in parks and large gardens have been grafted onto the roots of other oaks. The part to which the desired tree is grafted is known as the 'stock', and it must be closely related or else the graft will not take. The piece to be added to the stock is called the 'scion'.

The essential factor in grafting is the matching of the stock and the scion while they are growing rapidly – preferably in the spring. They are bound in place and covered to prevent their drying up or becoming diseased. By grafting, vigorously growing trees can be produced much more quickly than from seed.

Like most oaks, the Hungarian oak needs plenty of space in which to grow and it thrives on all but very wet soils. Sometimes fallen oak trees have been covered by encroaching bogs and impregnated with chemicals, which act as a preservative. They are then found as 'bog oak', and their dark, almost black timber is extremely hard and heavy. Acorns from most oak trees are sweet and form a valuable food for various animals. The acorns of the Hungarian oak have the additional quality of being suitable for grinding into a form of coffee.

Location

Date

Habitat

Sketches

The acorns are half-enclosed in a mossy 'cup'. They ripen at the end of their second year.

The underside of the leaf has felted, greyish-white hairs.

First-year acorns

The small leaves are alternate, with triangular, sharp-pointed lobes. They are shiny green on top. Acorns grow singly or in pairs, on a short stalk.

This evergreen oak has an open crown. It grows to 90 ft (27 m).

Sites Guide

This natural hybrid has been widely planted in parks and gardens. Its corky bark is usually a light, creamy brown.

It may be seen at sites numbers: 4-6, 17, 26, 28, 31 and 46.

Lucombe oak *Quercus × hispanica*

The original Lucombe oak was felled by the man after whom it was named, to provide wood for his own coffin; and for many years before his death at the age of 102 he kept the boards beneath his bed. In the 1760s, Mr Lucombe – an Exeter nurseryman – discovered that the oak, a cross between Turkey and cork oaks, occurred naturally when the two parent trees grew together. He raised a number of seedlings from the acorns of Turkey oak in his nursery, and noticed one that retained its leaves in the winter like the cork oaks; this he called 'evergreen Turkey oak'. He propagated thousands of trees from it by making grafts onto ordinary Turkey oaks.

In 1792, seedlings were raised from the acorns of the Lucombe oak itself, but being a hybrid they were variable in form. Some of these were also selected and propagated by grafts. They vary in bark thickness and the extent to which they retain their leaves.

The Lucombe oak – also known as the Spanish oak – retains the timber qualities of cork oak, being of dense texture with a good close grain. But it is not a commercial timber, and trees are only grown individually, for ornamental purposes.

Location

Date

Habitat

Sketches

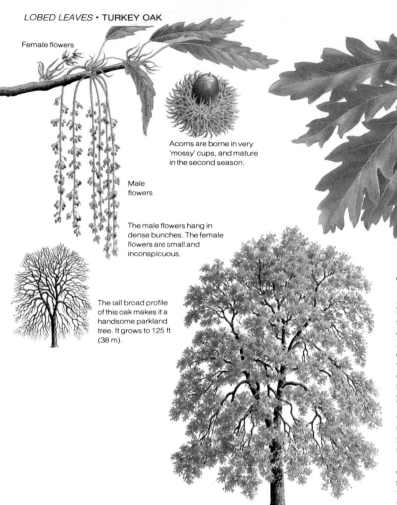

Female flowers

Acorns are borne in very 'mossy' cups, and mature in the second season.

Male flowers

The male flowers hang in dense bunches. The female flowers are small and inconspicuous.

The tall broad profile of this oak makes it a handsome parkland tree. It grows to 125 ft (38 m).

Leaves are alternate, with deeply cut lobes. They are rough, dark green and shiny on top. Stipules occur around the leaf base.

SITES GUIDE

This introduced tree grows more vigorously, and with more fissured and rougher bark, than native oaks.

It may be seen at sites numbers: 6, 7, 16, 17, 26, 29, 32-34, 42, 46, 47.

Turkey oak *Quercus cerris*

An earlier name for Turkey oak was wainscot oak, its timber being considered suitable only for making wall panelling. The tree was introduced from Turkey in the second half of the 19th century, when its timber was recommended for all kinds of uses. But it did not live up to expectations. Although the tree grows quickly and has a straight trunk, the timber is of poor quality. It warps easily, distorts, and is liable to split during seasoning. It cannot be used out-of-doors, as it quickly decays, so it was relegated to the role of lining and decorating living rooms and parlours.

The tree was also once known as iron oak, because of the weight of its timber when green; or mossy-cupped oak, from the distinctive acorn cups which hold the bitter acorns until they ripen in the second year. The acorns are freely produced, and the tree has become naturalised in many parts of southern Britain.

Turkey oak makes a distinctive ornamental tree and, unlike other oaks, it grows well on chalky soil. It is often used as the stock onto which other ornamental oaks are grafted. The tree is very late in losing its leaves in autumn, and in younger trees they persist throughout the winter in a withered state.

Location

Date

Habitat

Sketches

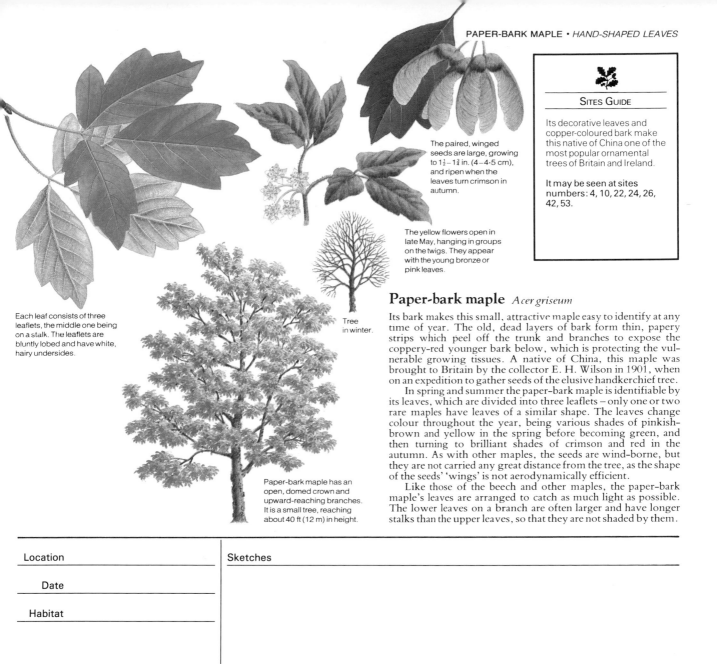

The paired, winged seeds are large, growing to 1½–1¾ in. (4–4·5 cm), and ripen when the leaves turn crimson in autumn.

The yellow flowers open in late May, hanging in groups on the twigs. They appear with the young bronze or pink leaves.

Each leaf consists of three leaflets, the middle one being on a stalk. The leaflets are bluntly lobed and have white, hairy undersides.

Tree in winter.

Paper-bark maple has an open, domed crown and upward-reaching branches. It is a small tree, reaching about 40 ft (12 m) in height.

Sites Guide

Its decorative leaves and copper-coloured bark make this native of China one of the most popular ornamental trees of Britain and Ireland.

It may be seen at sites numbers: 4, 10, 22, 24, 26, 42, 53.

Paper-bark maple *Acer griseum*

Its bark makes this small, attractive maple easy to identify at any time of year. The old, dead layers of bark form thin, papery strips which peel off the trunk and branches to expose the coppery-red younger bark below, which is protecting the vulnerable growing tissues. A native of China, this maple was brought to Britain by the collector E. H. Wilson in 1901, when on an expedition to gather seeds of the elusive handkerchief tree.

In spring and summer the paper-bark maple is identifiable by its leaves, which are divided into three leaflets – only one or two rare maples have leaves of a similar shape. The leaves change colour throughout the year, being various shades of pinkish-brown and yellow in the spring before becoming green, and then turning to brilliant shades of crimson and red in the autumn. As with other maples, the seeds are wind-borne, but they are not carried any great distance from the tree, as the shape of the seeds' 'wings' is not aerodynamically efficient.

Like those of the beech and other maples, the paper-bark maple's leaves are arranged to catch as much light as possible. The lower leaves on a branch are often larger and have longer stalks than the upper leaves, so that they are not shaded by them.

Location

Date

Habitat

Sketches

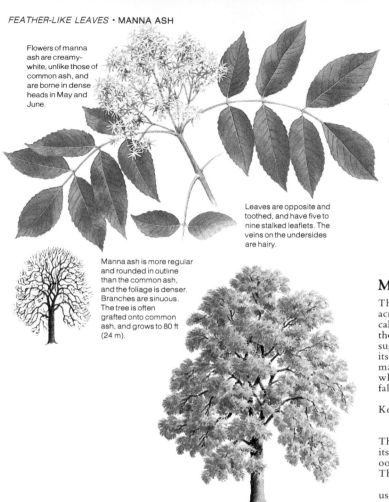

Flowers of manna ash are creamy-white, unlike those of common ash, and are borne in dense heads in May and June.

Leaves are opposite and toothed, and have five to nine stalked leaflets. The veins on the undersides are hairy.

Manna ash is more regular and rounded in outline than the common ash, and the foliage is denser. Branches are sinuous. The tree is often grafted onto common ash, and grows to 80 ft (24 m).

The single seeds have a slender wing and hang in dense bunches, turning brown in autumn.

SITES GUIDE

This decorative tree from the south of Europe is often planted in city parks for its early summer flowers.

It may be seen at sites numbers: 2, 7, 12, 33, 43.

Manna ash *Fraxinus ornus*

The Bible tells how the Children of Israel, escaping from Egypt across the Sinai Desert, were kept alive by a miraculous food, called manna, that fell from the sky (Exodus 16). It was once thought that the biblical manna might have been the viscous, sugary gum obtained from the manna ash, which accounts for its name. But as ash trees do not grow in desert regions, the manna is more likely to have been a desert lichen called *lecanora* which, dried to a powder by the sun and blown by the wind, falls to the ground in the form of whitish, edible flakes.

But it was probably the exudation of the manna to which Keats was referring in his poem *La Belle Dame Sans Merci*

'She found me roots of relish sweet,
And honey wild and manna–dew.'

The manna ash is still cultivated in southern Italy and Sicily for its gum. Shallow cuts are made in the branches and from these oozes pale yellow gum, which hardens on contact with the air. The gum is made into a syrup that is used as a mild laxative.

In Britain, where it was introduced in 1700, the manna ash is usually grafted onto a rootstock of common ash whose growth rate is much faster; differences in the bark show up the union.

Location

Date

Habitat

Sketches

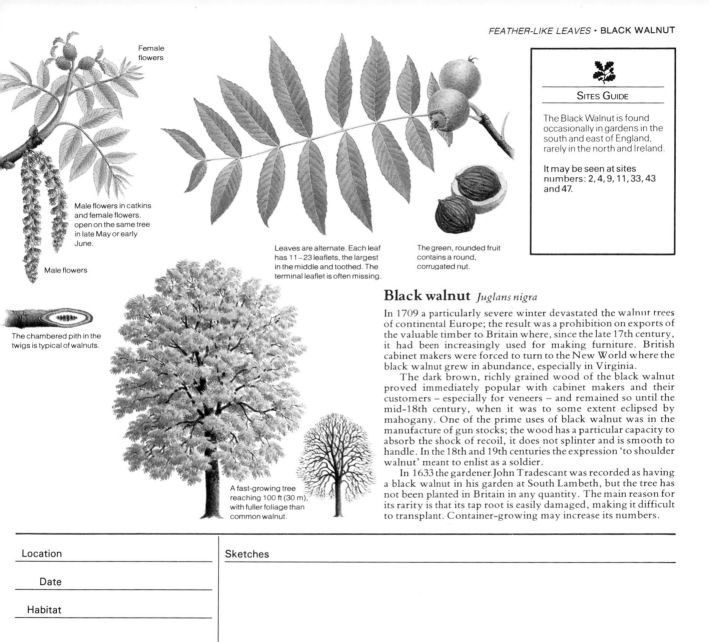

Female flowers

Male flowers in catkins and female flowers, open on the same tree in late May or early June.

Male flowers

The chambered pith in the twigs is typical of walnuts.

Leaves are alternate. Each leaf has 11–23 leaflets, the largest in the middle and toothed. The terminal leaflet is often missing.

The green, rounded fruit contains a round, corrugated nut.

A fast-growing tree reaching 100 ft (30 m), with fuller foliage than common walnut.

SITES GUIDE

The Black Walnut is found occasionally in gardens in the south and east of England, rarely in the north and Ireland.

It may be seen at sites numbers: 2, 4, 9, 11, 33, 43 and 47.

Black walnut *Juglans nigra*

In 1709 a particularly severe winter devastated the walnut trees of continental Europe; the result was a prohibition on exports of the valuable timber to Britain where, since the late 17th century, it had been increasingly used for making furniture. British cabinet makers were forced to turn to the New World where the black walnut grew in abundance, especially in Virginia.

The dark brown, richly grained wood of the black walnut proved immediately popular with cabinet makers and their customers – especially for veneers – and remained so until the mid-18th century, when it was to some extent eclipsed by mahogany. One of the prime uses of black walnut was in the manufacture of gun stocks; the wood has a particular capacity to absorb the shock of recoil, it does not splinter and is smooth to handle. In the 18th and 19th centuries the expression 'to shoulder walnut' meant to enlist as a soldier.

In 1633 the gardener John Tradescant was recorded as having a black walnut in his garden at South Lambeth, but the tree has not been planted in Britain in any quantity. The main reason for its rarity is that its tap root is easily damaged, making it difficult to transplant. Container-growing may increase its numbers.

Location

Date

Habitat

Sketches

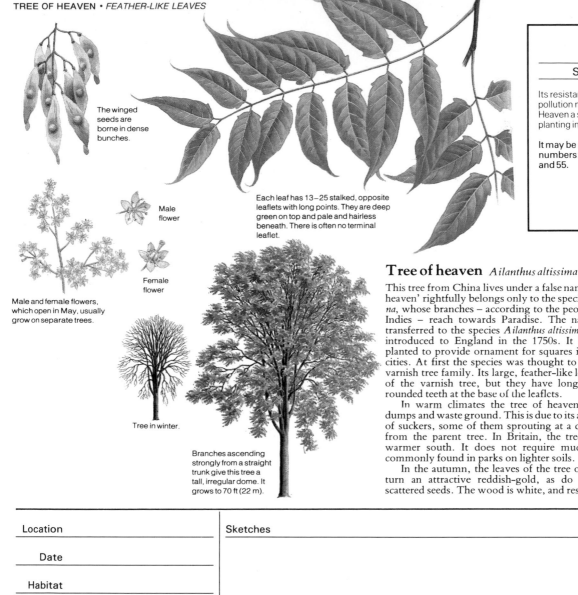

The winged seeds are borne in dense bunches.

Male flower

Female flower

Male and female flowers, which open in May, usually grow on separate trees.

Each leaf has 13–25 stalked, opposite leaflets with long points. They are deep green on top and pale and hairless beneath. There is often no terminal leaflet.

Tree in winter.

Branches ascending strongly from a straight trunk give this tree a tall, irregular dome. It grows to 70 ft (22 m).

Tree of heaven *Ailanthus altissima*

This tree from China lives under a false name. The name 'tree of heaven' rightfully belongs only to the species *Ailanthus molucca-na*, whose branches – according to the people of its native East Indies – reach towards Paradise. The name was, however, transferred to the species *Ailanthus altissima* when this tree was introduced to England in the 1750s. It has frequently been planted to provide ornament for squares in London and other cities. At first the species was thought to be a member of the varnish tree family. Its large, feather-like leaves resemble those of the varnish tree, but they have longer stalks and larger rounded teeth at the base of the leaflets.

In warm climates the tree of heaven spreads rapidly on dumps and waste ground. This is due to its abundant production of suckers, some of them sprouting at a considerable distance from the parent tree. In Britain, the tree grows best in the warmer south. It does not require much moisture, and is commonly found in parks on lighter soils.

In the autumn, the leaves of the tree of heaven sometimes turn an attractive reddish–gold, as do the twisted, wind-scattered seeds. The wood is white, and resembles ash.

Location

Date

Habitat

Sketches

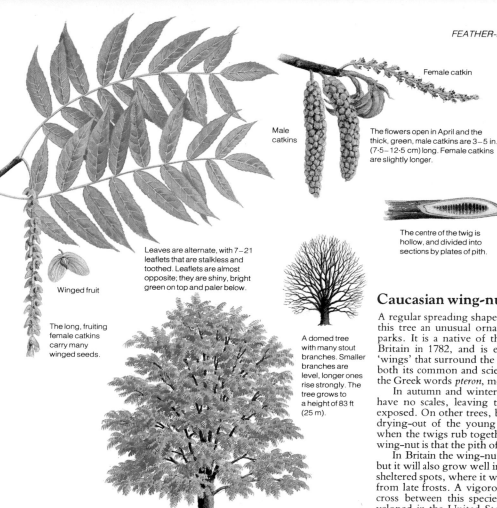

Female catkin

Male catkins

The flowers open in April and the thick, green, male catkins are 3–5 in. (7·5–12·5 cm) long. Female catkins are slightly longer.

The centre of the twig is hollow, and divided into sections by plates of pith.

Winged fruit

Leaves are alternate, with 7–21 leaflets that are stalkless and toothed. Leaflets are almost opposite; they are shiny, bright green on top and paler below.

The long, fruiting female catkins carry many winged seeds.

A domed tree with many stout branches. Smaller branches are level, longer ones rise strongly. The tree grows to a height of 83 ft (25 m).

SITES GUIDE

This fast-growing but uncommon tree flourishes near water. It grows best in southern Britain and Ireland.

It may be seen at sites numbers: 12, 27, 45, 47, 54.

Caucasian wing-nut *Pterocarya fraxinifolia*

A regular spreading shape and handsome ash–like foliage make this tree an unusual ornamental species in large gardens and parks. It is a native of the Caucasus that was introduced to Britain in 1782, and is easily identified by the round green 'wings' that surround the nuts, a feature from which it derives both its common and scientific names. *Pterocarya* comes from the Greek words *pteron*, meaning 'nut', and *karyon*, 'a wing'.

In autumn and winter the tree has distinctive buds which have no scales, leaving the undeveloped leaves and flowers exposed. On other trees, bud scales provide protection against drying-out of the young leaves, and against damage caused when the twigs rub together in a wind. Another feature of the wing–nut is that the pith of the twigs is divided into chambers.

In Britain the wing–nut thrives in damp areas near streams, but it will also grow well in other places. It needs to be grown in sheltered spots, where it will benefit from maximum protection from late frosts. A vigorous hybrid – *Pterocarya* × *rehderana*, a cross between this species and Chinese wing-nut – was developed in the United States in 1879, and was introduced to Britain in 1902.

Location

Date

Habitat

Sketches

Leaves are alternate. Each has 11–15 stalked leaflets, oval and hairless with small spines at their tips; they are bluish-green beneath.

In autumn, smooth brown pods split to release black seeds, shaped like kidneys. The pods remain hanging on the tree in bunches into the winter.

Pea-like flowers hang in sweet-scented clusters.

Locust tree *Robinia pseudoacacia*

Double confusion surrounds the locust tree, or false acacia. In the first place, the 'locusts' upon which John the Baptist is said to have fed in the wilderness were probably the fruits of the carob, or locust bean – not of this locust tree, which belongs to a different genus. The two trees acquired similar popular names because their pods are alike. Furthermore, neither tree has anything to do with locusts – in the eastern Mediterranean the same Greek word came to be used for the insect and for the carob pod simply because they looked somewhat alike.

Nowadays, the locust tree is less common in England than it was in the first half of the 19th century. At that time the radical journalist William Cobbett, author of *The English Gardener*, advocated the use of its hard wood for the pegs once used to fasten together the timbers of ships. Cobbett made a handsome profit by buying the trees from nurserymen and selling them to planters and speculators; but by the time they were ready for exploitation, iron was superseding timber in shipbuilding.

The tree's generic name honours the 17th-century gardener Jean Robin, who obtained seeds of the tree from America and grew trees from them in the Jardin des Plantes in Paris.

The crown of the locust tree, with its twisting branches, is broad and open. It grows to 83 ft (25 m).

Location	Sketches
Date	
Habitat	

Leaflets are greyish-green, and have teeth only on their upper halves. The leaf-stalk is red. White flowers appear in spreading heads in May.

White or purplish berries distinguish this tree from other rowans in autumn and winter. Earlier the berries are pale green.

The Hupeh rowan is a small tree up to 40 ft (12 m) tall, common in parks.

SITES GUIDE

The Hupeh Rowan, introduced from western China in 1910, is a vigorously growing tree that thrives in urban surroundings.

It may be seen at sites numbers: 13, 15, 38, 42.

Hupeh rowan *Sorbus hupehensis*

A colourful tree growing in the mountainous areas of China's Hupeh province caught the eye of a British plant collector, E. H. Wilson, in the early 1900s, and was introduced to this country as the Hupeh rowan. It makes an attractive display for most of the year. The leaves are a striking red in autumn, and the silver-grey summer foliage singles out the tree from other rowans.

In the autumn, in contrast with the red leaves, the rather pendulous berries turn from pale green to white or purplish-white and acquire a distinctive porcelain-like appearance. The berries do not seem to be as palatable to birds as those of other rowans, as they are not stripped so rapidly from the tree.

The Hupeh rowan is very suitable for lining urban streets. It is modest in size, and has fairly sparse foliage that does not accumulate in masses on the ground when it falls. The tree retains a pleasing shape at all seasons, without the need for pruning. It withstands drought and heat well, and therefore tolerates town surroundings where paving reduces the amount of water available and heat is reflected from buildings and roads. The Hupeh rowan also tolerates pollution, thriving in a contaminated atmosphere.

Location

Date

Habitat

Sketches

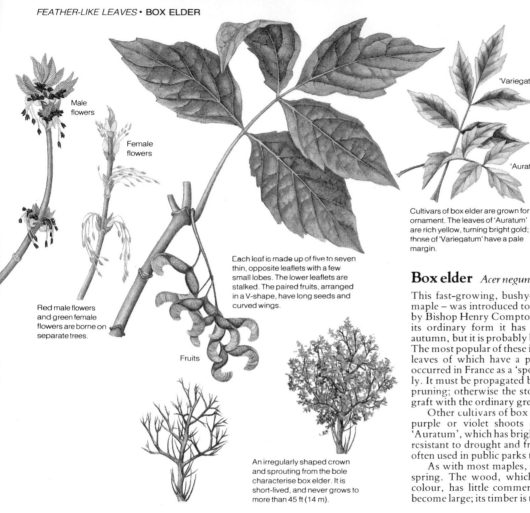

Male flowers

Female flowers

Red male flowers and green female flowers are borne on separate trees.

Each leaf is made up of five to seven thin, opposite leaflets with a few small lobes. The lower leaflets are stalked. The paired fruits, arranged in a V-shape, have long seeds and curved wings.

Fruits

An irregularly shaped crown and sprouting from the bole characterise box elder. It is short-lived, and never grows to more than 45 ft (14 m).

'Variegatum'

'Auratum'

Cultivars of box elder are grown for ornament. The leaves of 'Auratum' are rich yellow, turning bright gold; those of 'Variegatum' have a pale margin.

SITES GUIDE

This fast-growing native of North America has greyish-brown bark, which cracks into fissures with age.

It may be seen at sites numbers: 12, 22, 26.

Box elder *Acer negundo*

This fast-growing, bushy-headed tree – also called ash-leaved maple – was introduced to Britain from North America in 1688 by Bishop Henry Compton, an avid collector of exotic trees. In its ordinary form it has green leaves which turn yellow in autumn, but it is probably better known for its various cultivars. The most popular of these is a variegated form 'Variegatum', the leaves of which have a pale margin. This cultivar originally occurred in France as a 'sport', or aberrant form arising natural-ly. It must be propagated by grafting and maintained by regular pruning; otherwise the stock sends up shoots and replaces the graft with the ordinary green form.

Other cultivars of box elder include 'Violaceum', which has purple or violet shoots covered with a white bloom, and 'Auratum', which has bright, golden-yellow leaves. Box elder is resistant to drought and frost, and because it grows so fast it is often used in public parks to screen unsightly features.

As with most maples, sugar can be obtained from the sap in spring. The wood, which is light, soft and creamy-white in colour, has little commercial value because the tree does not become large; its timber is therefore available only in small sizes.

Location

Date

Habitat

Sketches

Female flowers

Male flowers

Male and female flowers grow on separate trees. Males appear as small green catkins, females are small, stalked, round and knob-like.

In autumn, foliage turns amber coloured before falling.

Leaves are two-lobed and fan-shaped, with radiating veins reflecting the leaf shape. The fruits resemble small green plums on long stalks.

A tall, slender trunk and drooping foliage consisting of distinctively fan-shaped leaves identify this tree, which can reach a height of 100 ft (30 m).

SITES GUIDE

The tumbling foliage of this relic of primeval forests can still grace parks and gardens in south and south-west England.

It may be seen at sites numbers: 3, 7, 12, 17-19, 22, 28, 34, 38, 39, 42, 43.

Maidenhair tree *Ginkgo biloba*

Fossils of the maidenhair tree have been found in coal seams formed 250 million years ago, yet this ancient, primitive tree lives on today, the sole survivor of its family. It is unique in other ways too. Fertilisation is by free-swimming male sperm which reach the ovules through a film of water – a method found in ferns, but in no other tree living today. The unusual, fan-shaped leaves – partly divided in the middle and with parallel veins – resemble the maidenhair fern and give the tree its common name.

The tree survived through the centuries by cultivation in temple and palace gardens in China; its generic name *Ginkgo* is said to be derived from the Chinese *yin kuo*, meaning the 'silver fruit' that the tree sometimes bears. It was introduced to Europe early in the 18th century, and has also been extensively planted in America as a street tree.

In a dry autumn, the leaves turn a brilliant amber before falling to expose the short, blunt twigs which, in winter, give the maidenhair the appearance of a pear tree. The pale yellow wood is light, lacking in strength and without commercial use. In Japan the hard fruits are roasted and eaten as a hangover cure.

Location

Date

Habitat

Sketches

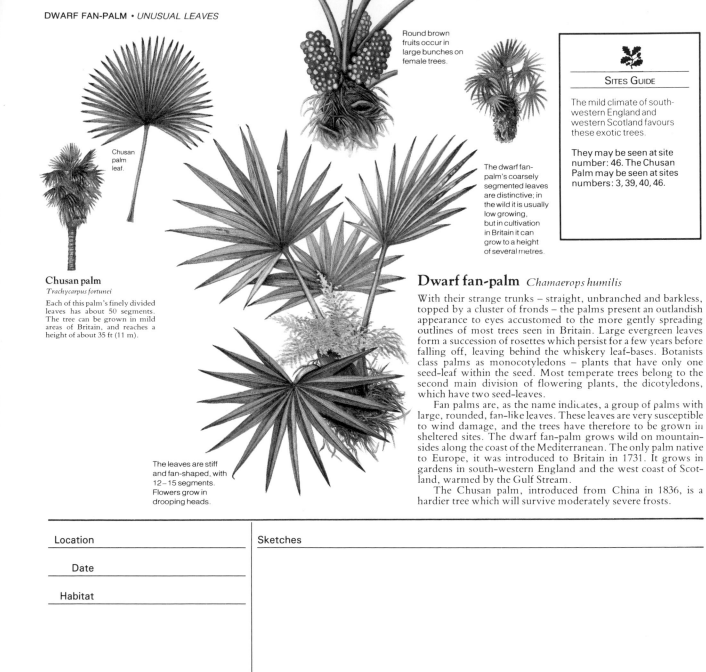

Chusan palm leaf.

Round brown fruits occur in large bunches on female trees.

The dwarf fan-palm's coarsely segmented leaves are distinctive; in the wild it is usually low growing, but in cultivation in Britain it can grow to a height of several metres.

Chusan palm
Trachycarpus fortunei

Each of this palm's finely divided leaves has about 50 segments. The tree can be grown in mild areas of Britain, and reaches a height of about 35 ft (11 m).

The leaves are stiff and fan-shaped, with 12–15 segments. Flowers grow in drooping heads.

SITES GUIDE

The mild climate of south-western England and western Scotland favours these exotic trees.

They may be seen at site number: 46. The Chusan Palm may be seen at sites numbers: 3, 39, 40, 46.

Dwarf fan-palm *Chamaerops humilis*

With their strange trunks – straight, unbranched and barkless, topped by a cluster of fronds – the palms present an outlandish appearance to eyes accustomed to the more gently spreading outlines of most trees seen in Britain. Large evergreen leaves form a succession of rosettes which persist for a few years before falling off, leaving behind the whiskery leaf-bases. Botanists class palms as monocotyledons – plants that have only one seed-leaf within the seed. Most temperate trees belong to the second main division of flowering plants, the dicotyledons, which have two seed-leaves.

Fan palms are, as the name indicates, a group of palms with large, rounded, fan-like leaves. These leaves are very susceptible to wind damage, and the trees have therefore to be grown in sheltered sites. The dwarf fan-palm grows wild on mountainsides along the coast of the Mediterranean. The only palm native to Europe, it was introduced to Britain in 1731. It grows in gardens in south-western England and the west coast of Scotland, warmed by the Gulf Stream.

The Chusan palm, introduced from China in 1836, is a hardier tree which will survive moderately severe frosts.

Location	Sketches
Date	
Habitat	

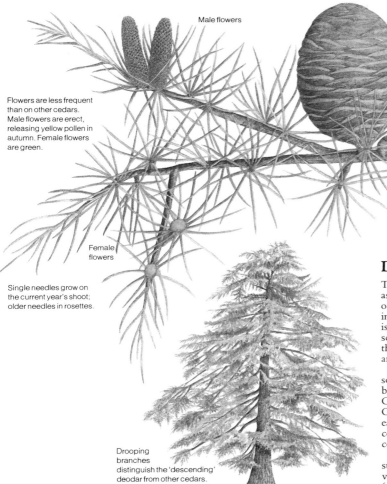

Male flowers

Flowers are less frequent than on other cedars. Male flowers are erect, releasing yellow pollen in autumn. Female flowers are green.

Female flowers

Single needles grow on the current year's shoot; older needles in rosettes.

Large, barrel-shaped erect cones ripen in two years, then break up to leave a central spike.

Drooping branches distinguish the 'descending' deodar from other cedars. It grows to 110 ft (33 m).

SITES GUIDE

The Deodar differs from other cedars in its paler green foliage, with longer, softer needles, and triangular overall shape.

It may be seen at sites numbers: 1, 5, 6, 17, 22, 26, 27, 30, 31, 34, 36, 42, 43, 46, 47 and 48.

Deodar *Cedrus deodara*

This native of the snow slopes of the Himalayas has religious associations in its native land, where it is also known as the 'tree of God' or the 'sacred Indian fir'. Like other cedars, it is regarded in India as a symbol of fruitfulness and durability, and the timber is traditionally used for building temples and palaces. Its fragrant scent makes it an attractive timber for construction work, though it is also used more prosaically to make railway sleepers and bridges.

This shapely conifer was introduced to Britain in 1831 and soon found favour as an ornamental tree; many specimens may be seen in gardens, parks, churchyards and graveyards. The Commissioners for Crown Lands, forerunners of the Forestry Commission, experimented with the deodar as a forest tree as early as 1860. This was one of many attempts to add a new coniferous timber species to the few conifers then available for commercial purposes in Britain.

The experiment showed, however, that the deodar was not suitable for commercial forestry in Britain, as it comes from a very different climate. Trees from these plantings survive in a few Crown forests, such as the New Forest.

Location

Date

Habitat

Sketches

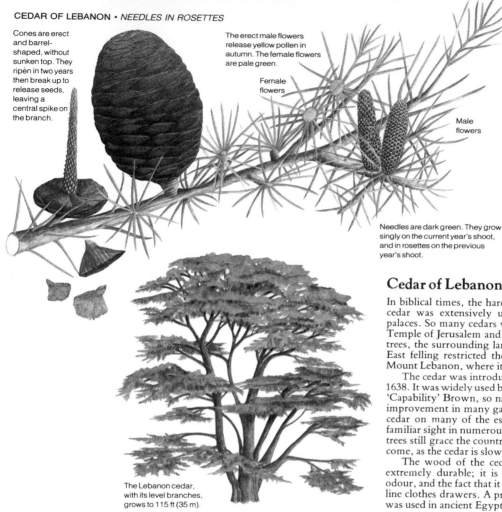

Cones are erect and barrel-shaped, without sunken top. They ripen in two years then break up to release seeds, leaving a central spike on the branch.

The erect male flowers release yellow pollen in autumn. The female flowers are pale green.

Female flowers

Male flowers

Needles are dark green. They grow singly on the current year's shoot, and in rosettes on the previous year's shoot.

The Lebanon cedar, with its level branches, grows to 115 ft (35 m).

SITES GUIDE

Many of these magnificent trees survive today from extensive planting during the 18th and 19th centuries.

They may be seen at sites numbers: 6, 8, 10-12, 14, 18, 20-22, 24-32, 36, 39, 46, 47.

Cedar of Lebanon *Cedrus libani*

In biblical times, the hard and enduring wood of the Lebanon cedar was extensively used in the building of temples and palaces. So many cedars were felled for the construction of the Temple of Jerusalem and Solomon's Palace that, stripped of its trees, the surrounding landscape became a desert. In the Near East felling restricted the cedar to a relatively small area, on Mount Lebanon, where it is now preserved.

The cedar was introduced to Britain as an ornamental tree in 1638. It was widely used by the 18th-century landscape gardener 'Capability' Brown, so named because he saw a 'capability' for improvement in many gardens. Brown planted the flat-topped cedar on many of the estates he redesigned, and it became a familiar sight in numerous parks and large gardens. Many of his trees still grace the countryside, and will do so for some time to come, as the cedar is slow-growing and long-lived.

The wood of the cedar of Lebanon is dense, strong and extremely durable; it is also sweetly scented. Because of its odour, and the fact that it is resistant to insects, it is often used to line clothes drawers. A preservative oil distilled from the wood was used in ancient Egypt to embalm the dead.

Location

Date

Habitat

Sketches

Needles, like those of cedar of Lebanon, are blue-green or dark green, growing singly on the current year's shoot and in rosettes on the previous year's shoot.

Female flowers

Pinkish male flowers and green female flowers appear in autumn.

Male flowers

The tree can best be distinguished from other cedars by its rising branches, making it easy to remember as 'Atlas: ascending'. It grows to 120 ft (36 m).

Cone is shaped like a wasp's nest with a sunken top. It ripens in two years then breaks up, leaving a central spike.

SITES GUIDE

In its native North Africa the Atlas Cedar is usually green, but in Britain and Ireland it often appears blue-green.

It may be seen at sites numbers: 1, 4, 6, 12, 15, 18, 22, 24, 27, 28, 30, 31, 33, 41, 43, 46-49.

Atlas cedar *Cedrus atlantica*

Most gardeners think of Atlas cedar as the 'blue cedar' because of the attractive blue-green foliage of some specimens. The 'blue' form occurs sporadically in the wild, but there the colour is not as vivid as in the ornamental species cultivated in British gardens. In its native North Africa, the cedar is confined to the Atlas mountains of Algeria and Morocco. It is regarded by some botanists as a western form of the cedar of Lebanon, which it closely resembles.

The Atlas cedar was introduced here in 1841 and grows on sandy soils, loam and limestone. It prefers hotter, drier conditions than most conifers. Fewer large Atlas cedars than cedars of Lebanon exist in Britain, for the Atlas cedar has been grown in this country for less than 150 years, while the first cedars of Lebanon were planted in Britain more than two centuries ago. Because the Atlas cedar reaches a height of around 120 ft (36 m) it needs plenty of space, and specimens planted in small gardens have to be felled before they are fully grown.

Unlike other conifers, the Atlas cedar flowers in autumn. Slug-shaped male catkins then fall in considerable numbers, and often puzzle people as to their origin.

Location

Date

Habitat

Sketches

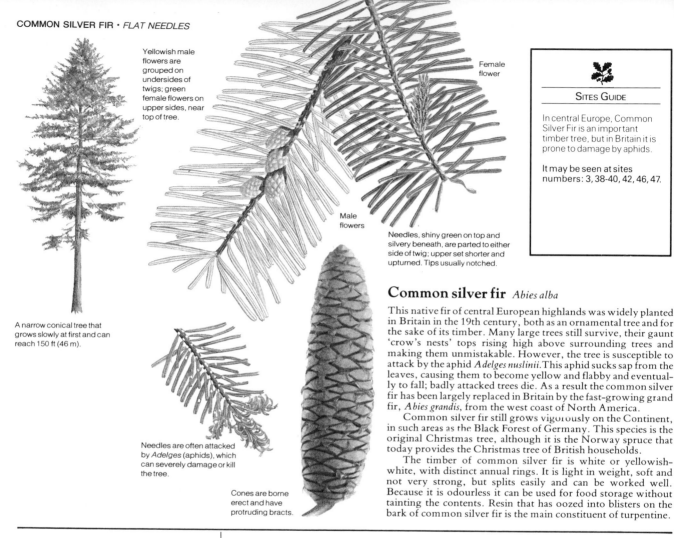

Yellowish male flowers are grouped on undersides of twigs; green female flowers on upper sides, near top of tree.

A narrow conical tree that grows slowly at first and can reach 150 ft (46 m).

Female flower

Male flowers

Needles, shiny green on top and silvery beneath, are parted to either side of twig; upper set shorter and upturned. Tips usually notched.

Needles are often attacked by *Adelges* (aphids), which can severely damage or kill the tree.

Cones are borne erect and have protruding bracts.

SITES GUIDE

In central Europe, Common Silver Fir is an important timber tree, but in Britain it is prone to damage by aphids.

It may be seen at sites numbers: 3, 38-40, 42, 46, 47.

Common silver fir *Abies alba*

This native fir of central European highlands was widely planted in Britain in the 19th century, both as an ornamental tree and for the sake of its timber. Many large trees still survive, their gaunt 'crow's nests' tops rising high above surrounding trees and making them unmistakable. However, the tree is susceptible to attack by the aphid *Adelges nuslinii*. This aphid sucks sap from the leaves, causing them to become yellow and flabby and eventually to fall; badly attacked trees die. As a result the common silver fir has been largely replaced in Britain by the fast-growing grand fir, *Abies grandis*, from the west coast of North America.

Common silver fir still grows vigorously on the Continent, in such areas as the Black Forest of Germany. This species is the original Christmas tree, although it is the Norway spruce that today provides the Christmas tree of British households.

The timber of common silver fir is white or yellowish-white, with distinct annual rings. It is light in weight, soft and not very strong, but splits easily and can be worked well. Because it is odourless it can be used for food storage without tainting the contents. Resin that has oozed into blisters on the bark of common silver fir is the main constituent of turpentine.

Location

Date

Habitat

Sketches

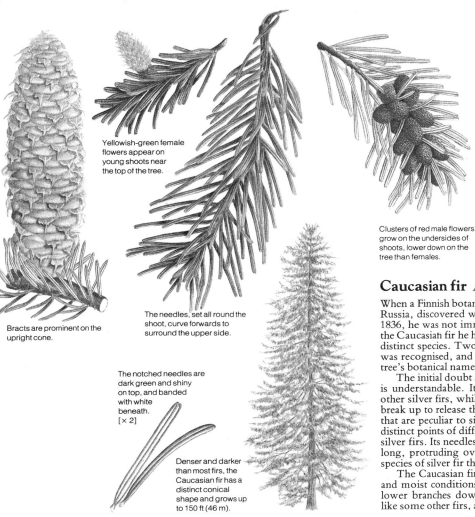

Yellowish-green female flowers appear on young shoots near the top of the tree.

Bracts are prominent on the upright cone.

The needles, set all round the shoot, curve forwards to surround the upper side.

The notched needles are dark green and shiny on top, and banded with white beneath. [× 2]

Denser and darker than most firs, the Caucasian fir has a distinct conical shape and grows up to 150 ft (46 m).

Clusters of red male flowers grow on the undersides of shoots, lower down on the tree than females.

Sites Guide

This stately and ornamental conifer grows well in Britain, though it is seldom seen outside the collections and parks.

It may be seen at sites numbers: 2, 10, 17, 27, 37, 42.

Caucasian fir *Abies nordmanniana*

When a Finnish botanist called Nordmann, working in southern Russia, discovered what was in fact a new species of silver fir in 1836, he was not immediately given the credit he deserved, for the Caucasian fir he had identified was not at first recognised as a distinct species. Two years later, however, its separate identity was recognised, and Nordmann's name was perpetuated in the tree's botanical name.

The initial doubt about Caucasian fir being a separate species is understandable. It has the regular outline characteristic of other silver firs, while its cones stand upright on the shoots and break up to release the seeds when they are ripe – both features that are peculiar to silver firs and to cedars. However, there are distinct points of difference between the Caucasian fir and other silver firs. Its needles are denser, and the bracts on the cones are long, protruding over the cone scales, whereas in some other species of silver fir they are short or completely hidden.

The Caucasian fir grows best in the British Isles in the cool and moist conditions of the west coast. In old age it retains its lower branches down to ground level, instead of losing them like some other firs, and its foliage remains thick.

Location

Date

Habitat

Sketches

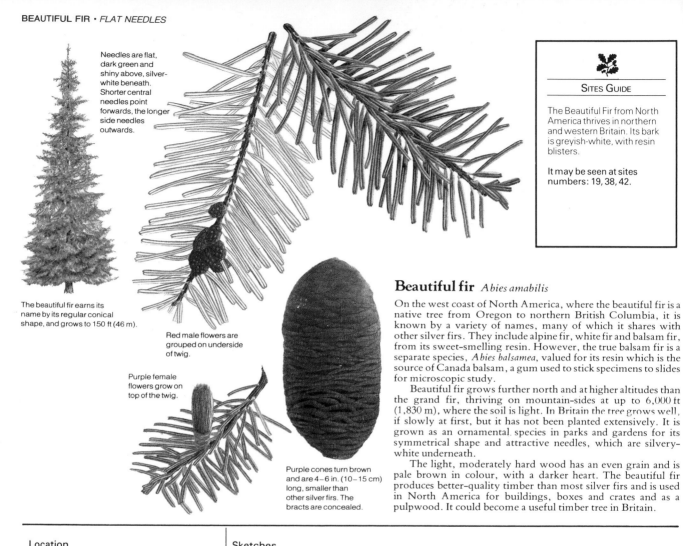

Needles are flat, dark green and shiny above, silver-white beneath. Shorter central needles point forwards, the longer side needles outwards.

The beautiful fir earns its name by its regular conical shape, and grows to 150 ft (46 m).

Red male flowers are grouped on underside of twig.

Purple female flowers grow on top of the twig.

Purple cones turn brown and are 4–6 in. (10–15 cm) long, smaller than other silver firs. The bracts are concealed.

SITES GUIDE

The Beautiful Fir from North America thrives in northern and western Britain. Its bark is greyish-white, with resin blisters.

It may be seen at sites numbers: 19, 38, 42.

Beautiful fir *Abies amabilis*

On the west coast of North America, where the beautiful fir is a native tree from Oregon to northern British Columbia, it is known by a variety of names, many of which it shares with other silver firs. They include alpine fir, white fir and balsam fir, from its sweet-smelling resin. However, the true balsam fir is a separate species, *Abies balsamea*, valued for its resin which is the source of Canada balsam, a gum used to stick specimens to slides for microscopic study.

Beautiful fir grows further north and at higher altitudes than the grand fir, thriving on mountain-sides at up to 6,000 ft (1,830 m), where the soil is light. In Britain the tree grows well, if slowly at first, but it has not been planted extensively. It is grown as an ornamental species in parks and gardens for its symmetrical shape and attractive needles, which are silvery-white underneath.

The light, moderately hard wood has an even grain and is pale brown in colour, with a darker heart. The beautiful fir produces better-quality timber than most silver firs and is used in North America for buildings, boxes and crates and as a pulpwood. It could become a useful timber tree in Britain.

Location

Date

Habitat

Sketches

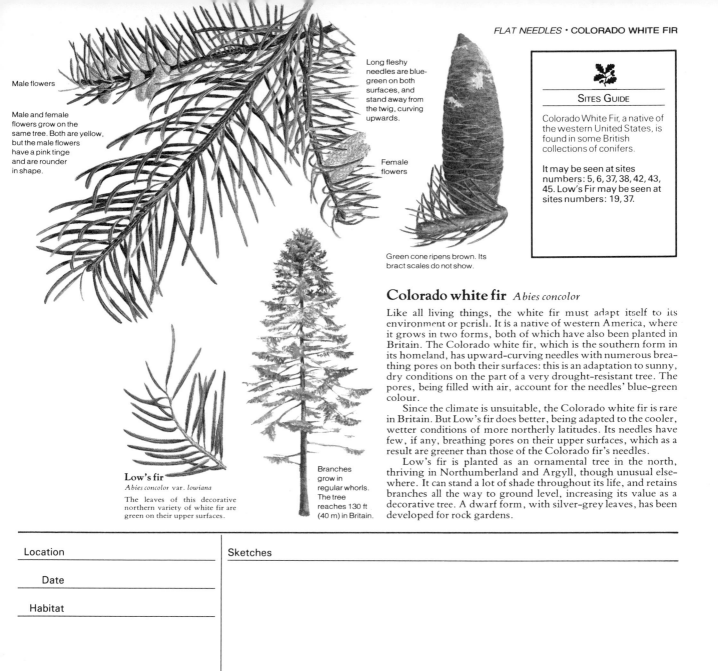

Male flowers

Male and female flowers grow on the same tree. Both are yellow, but the male flowers have a pink tinge and are rounder in shape.

Long fleshy needles are blue-green on both surfaces, and stand away from the twig, curving upwards.

Female flowers

Green cone ripens brown. Its bract scales do not show.

SITES GUIDE

Colorado White Fir, a native of the western United States, is found in some British collections of conifers.

It may be seen at sites numbers: 5, 6, 37, 38, 42, 43, 45. Low's Fir may be seen at sites numbers: 19, 37.

Low's fir

Abies concolor var. *lowiana*

The leaves of this decorative northern variety of white fir are green on their upper surfaces.

Branches grow in regular whorls. The tree reaches 130 ft (40 m) in Britain.

Colorado white fir *Abies concolor*

Like all living things, the white fir must adapt itself to its environment or perish. It is a native of western America, where it grows in two forms, both of which have also been planted in Britain. The Colorado white fir, which is the southern form in its homeland, has upward-curving needles with numerous breathing pores on both their surfaces: this is an adaptation to sunny, dry conditions on the part of a very drought-resistant tree. The pores, being filled with air, account for the needles' blue-green colour.

Since the climate is unsuitable, the Colorado white fir is rare in Britain. But Low's fir does better, being adapted to the cooler, wetter conditions of more northerly latitudes. Its needles have few, if any, breathing pores on their upper surfaces, which as a result are greener than those of the Colorado fir's needles.

Low's fir is planted as an ornamental tree in the north, thriving in Northumberland and Argyll, though unusual elsewhere. It can stand a lot of shade throughout its life, and retains branches all the way to ground level, increasing its value as a decorative tree. A dwarf form, with silver-grey leaves, has been developed for rock gardens.

Location

Date

Habitat

Sketches

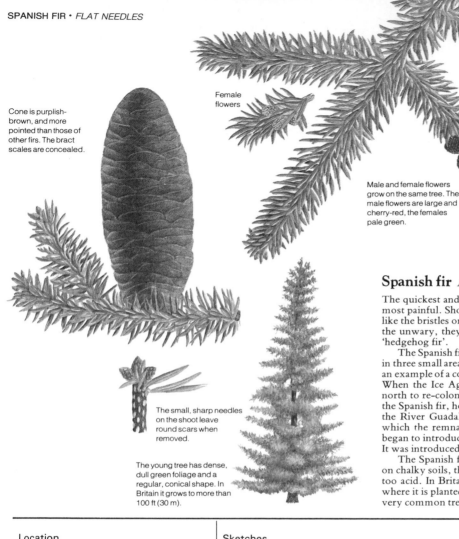

Cone is purplish-brown, and more pointed than those of other firs. The bract scales are concealed.

Female flowers

Male flowers

Male and female flowers grow on the same tree. The male flowers are large and cherry-red, the females pale green.

The small, sharp needles on the shoot leave round scars when removed.

The young tree has dense, dull green foliage and a regular, conical shape. In Britain it grows to more than 100 ft (30 m).

SITES GUIDE

Native to the Sierra Nevada mountains of Spain, this fir has a smooth, dark grey bark, which becomes roughened with age.

It may be seen at sites numbers: 22, 37, 38, 43, 48.

Spanish fir *Abies pinsapo*

The quickest and easiest way to identify a Spanish fir is also the most painful. Short, prickly needles spread all around the shoots like the bristles on a bottle-brush, and when they are grasped by the unwary, they show how the tree earned its other name of 'hedgehog fir'.

The Spanish fir is not a native of Britain, but grows wild only in three small areas in the Sierra Nevada mountains of Spain. It is an example of a conifer that was almost wiped out in the Ice Age. When the Ice Age finally retreated, vegetation moved slowly north to re-colonise the areas laid bare by the ice. The spread of the Spanish fir, however, was blocked by the east-west valley of the River Guadalquivir, and it was confined to the region in which the remnants of the native tree grow today, until men began to introduce it as an ornamental tree in gardens elsewhere. It was introduced into Britain in 1839.

The Spanish fir is one of the few silver firs that will flourish on chalky soils, though it does well on other soils if they are not too acid. In Britain it grows best in the warmer south and east where it is planted in parks, gardens and churchyards. It is not a very common tree, however, and grows slowly.

Location

Date

Habitat

Sketches

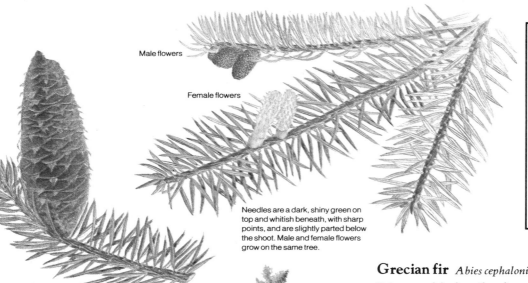

Male flowers

Female flowers

Needles are a dark, shiny green on top and whitish beneath, with sharp points, and are slightly parted below the shoot. Male and female flowers grow on the same tree.

Cone grows upright on the twig to about 6 in. (15 cm) long. Bract scales protrude and bend downwards.

This fir is broad and heavily branched. It is roughly conical, but often has a flattened top. It grows to 115 ft (35 m).

Grecian fir *Abies cephalonica*

Being one of the first silver firs to produce new leaves in spring, the Grecian fir is vulnerable to damage by frost. Once established, however, it grows quickly, and it is valued as an ornamental tree for gardens where there is space for its wide branches to spread. The Grecian fir was introduced to Britain in 1824 from the mountainous country of southern Greece. In its homeland the tree is today less widespread than it used to be, because of devastation by fire and grazing by animals.

The Grecian fir resembles the Spanish fir in having prickly leaves, though they are not quite so stiff. Both trees grow best on chalky soils, and will cross-pollinate naturally when growing close together. The original cross between the two trees, × *vilmorinii*, was brought about in 1868 by pollinating the flowers of the Spanish fir with pollen from the Grecian fir. The tree produced was intermediate in character, and grafts from this are sometimes found growing in collections.

The wood of Grecian fir is similar to that of other firs in being rather soft and not very strong or durable. Grecian fir has the additional drawback that its coarse branching produces many knots, which make weak points in the timber.

Location

Date

Habitat

Sketches

Turned-in edges of needles make them curve away from twig. Undersides of needles are brilliant white. Male flowers are reddish, females blue.

Female flower

Male flowers

Whorls of branches separated by lengths of stem give the tree a regular pyramid shape. One whorl and one stem length is a year's growth. The tree grows to 65 ft (20 m).

SITES GUIDE

The ornamental Delavay's Silver Fir adapts well to the British climate, but may be damaged by late frosts.

It may be seen at sites numbers: 10, 43, 45. Forrest's Fir may be seen at sites numbers: 10, 38, 42.

Forrest's fir
Abies delavayi var. *forrestii*

In this variety of Delavay's fir, the tips of the bracts protrude between the cone scales. The needles are less noticeably curved.

Inky blue, barrel-shaped cones appear early in the tree's life. The bracts do not protrude between the cone scales.

Delavay's silver fir *Abies delavayi*

More than one European plant collector risked death from disease, natural disaster or hostile inhabitants in western China in the 19th century, and the Frenchman Jean Marie Delavay (1834–95) was among the unluckiest. This Jesuit missionary was an avid hunter of new plants. His right arm became paralysed and he caught bubonic plague, from which he never fully recovered. But he never gave up his quest and he continued collecting until his death, still in China.

Delavay sent thousands of carefully dried plant specimens, seeds and young living plants, back to botanists in France but even then his bad luck continued. Many of the dried specimens were ruined after their arrival because they were not looked after properly, and most of the living plants were killed because they were treated as hot-house plants.

Delavay's silver fir grows in the mountains of China at altitudes of between 10,000 and 11,000 ft (3,050–3,400 m). Its attractive blue cones and the white undersides of the needles have made it a garden favourite. The variety most commonly grown in Britain, *forrestii*, was named after one of Delavay's successors – the Scotsman George Forrest (1873–1932).

Location

Date

Habitat

Sketches

Female flowers

Male flowers are deep red and cluster under twigs. Females are yellow, upright and shaped like a pastry brush.

Male flowers

Needles in shade are smaller and adhere to the twig.

Needles are blue-green on both sides. On the lower branches they lie close to the twig; in full light on the upper branches they are long and turn upwards.

Layers of horizontal branches form the regular outline of the noble fir. It grows to 150 ft (45 m).

Upwards curving needle from twig of upper branch.

Cones are very big and upright, with protruding, down-turned bracts. The cones break up to leave a thin, central spike.

Sites Guide

This imposing American native, occasionally planted for timber in Europe, is widely grown in British gardens.

It may be seen at sites numbers: 2, 10, 16, 19, 22, 24, 26, 37, 38, 42, 44, 47.

Noble fir *Abies procera*

In the mid-19th century the Scottish tree collector David Douglas introduced this aristocrat of the North American mountains to a new home in the 'policies', or ornamental woodlands surrounding Scottish mansions. It is now an established part of the Scottish landscape, standing firm against wind and snow on exposed northern sites even where the soil is poor. In the less-rugged south the noble fir often sickens and sometimes dies, attacked by a woolly aphis (*adelges*) which destroys the terminal bud. It also fares badly in the shade or on very chalky soils.

A striking feature of the noble fir is the huge, green cone, growing up to 10 in. (25 cm) long and nearly half as broad, with prominent, down-turned bracts. Some of the tree's alternative names refer to these bracts – the 'bracted fir' and the 'feather-cone fir'.

Because it withstands exposure, is resistant to snow damage and tolerates poor soil conditions, the noble fir has been planted as a timber tree, but not in sufficient quantities in Britain to make it commercially significant. However, the wood is light and fairly strong, with a hard, close grain, and in North America it is used for interior building work.

Location

Date

Habitat

Sketches

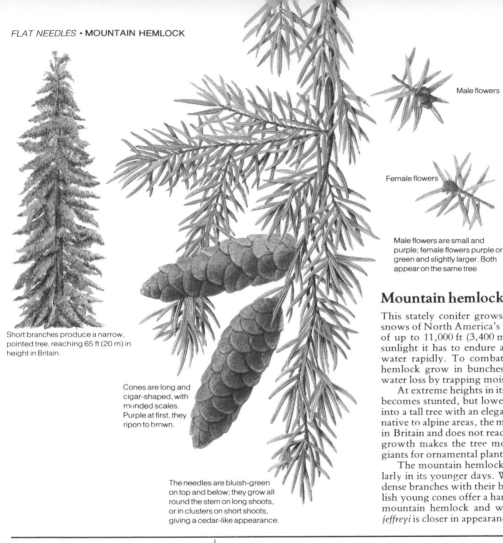

Short branches produce a narrow, pointed tree, reaching 65 ft (20 m) in height in Britain.

Cones are long and cigar-shaped, with rounded scales. Purple at first, they ripen to brown.

The needles are bluish-green on top and below; they grow all round the stem on long shoots, or in clusters on short shoots, giving a cedar-like appearance.

Male flowers

Female flowers

Male flowers are small and purple; female flowers purple or green and slightly larger. Both appear on the same tree

SITES GUIDE

Its decorative shape and blue-green foliage make this American tree an attractive rarity in British collections.

It may be seen at sites numbers: 19, 27, 30, 37, 43 and 45.

Mountain hemlock *Tsuga mertensiana*

This stately conifer grows on the very edge of the mountain snows of North America's western coast, taking root at heights of up to 11,000 ft (3,400 m). The rarefied air, gales and fierce sunlight it has to endure at such altitudes cause a tree to lose water rapidly. To combat this, the needles of the mountain hemlock grow in bunches, like those of cedars; this reduces water loss by trapping moisture vapour.

At extreme heights in its native home the mountain hemlock becomes stunted, but lower down the mountain-sides it grows into a tall tree with an elegantly narrow profile. Like other trees native to alpine areas, the mountain hemlock grows only slowly in Britain and does not reach a great height. Although this slow growth makes the tree more suitable than some of the forest giants for ornamental planting, it is still not widely grown.

The mountain hemlock will tolerate a lot of shade, particularly in its younger days. When grown in the open its shapely, dense branches with their bunched, grey–blue needles and purplish young cones offer a handsome spectacle. A hybrid between mountain hemlock and western hemlock known as *Tsuga × jeffreyi* is closer in appearance to its mountain hemlock parent.

Location

Date

Habitat

Sketches

The cones are smaller than those of western hemlock, and borne on short stalks.

Female flowers

Male flowers

On twig's upper surface the central row of needles is twisted, showing white undersides. Male flowers are yellow; females are green.

The needles taper from their base to a blunt end. [× 2]

This bushy tree's many-forked stem and its broad, dense, conical crown are distinctive. It grows to a height of 105 ft (32 m).

SITES GUIDE

Not used in Britain as a timber tree, Eastern Hemlock is popular in parks, particularly in eastern England.

It may be seen at sites numbers: 13, 14, 16, 17, 19, 30, 34, 37, 41, 45, 48.

Eastern hemlock *Tsuga canadensis*

In 1736 Peter Collinson, an amateur collector with a garden in London, introduced to Britain the eastern hemlock from the east coast of North America. Although it is hardier and will grow at higher altitudes than the western hemlock, a later introduction, it does not grow so well in Britain as its relative. Moreover, it forks profusely as it grows, so that it is unsuitable as a timber tree. In North America this forking is not typical of the tree, so that its timber can be used there for construction work as well as for making paper pulp.

In Britain, the eastern hemlock's habit of forking is turned to advantage, for this makes it an effective ornamental tree. Many bushy dwarf forms have been developed for decorative use, especially for rockeries and trough gardens. The tree has the advantage, too, that it will grow on soils over chalk, so long as there is adequate moisture.

The leaves of the hemlocks are very like those of the yew in shape, leading to their being given the generic name *Tsuga*, a Japanese word meaning 'yew-like'. European botanists so named the genus because the first member of it to be discovered was the Japanese hemlock.

Location

Date

Habitat

Sketches

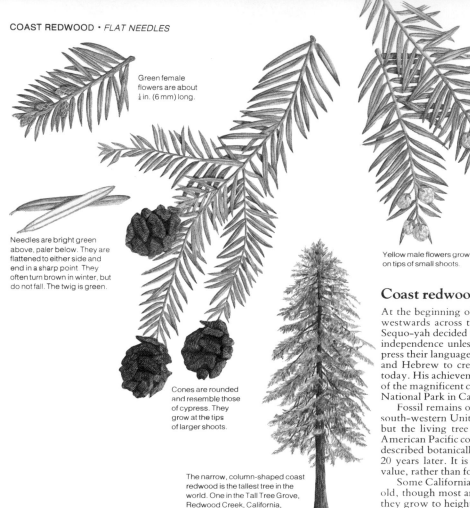

Green female flowers are about ¼ in. (6 mm) long.

Needles are bright green above, paler below. They are flattened to either side and end in a sharp point. They often turn brown in winter, but do not fall. The twig is green.

Cones are rounded and resemble those of cypress. They grow at the tips of larger shoots.

The narrow, column-shaped coast redwood is the tallest tree in the world. One in the Tall Tree Grove, Redwood Creek, California, measures almost 368 ft (112 m).

Yellow male flowers grow on tips of small shoots.

SITES GUIDE

Long-lived Coast Redwoods from California have been planted in many British parks and gardens.

They may be seen at sites numbers: 4, 5, 8, 10, 14, 16, 17, 19, 23, 27, 31, 42, 47, 49 and 51.

Coast redwood *Sequoia sempervirens*

At the beginning of the 19th century, as white settlers moved westwards across the United States, a Cherokee Indian called Sequo-yah decided that his people could not hope to retain their independence unless they developed a written alphabet to express their language. Sequo-yah borrowed from English, Greek and Hebrew to create a Cherokee alphabet that is still in use today. His achievement is commemorated in the scientific name of the magnificent coast redwood and in the name of the Sequoia National Park in California.

Fossil remains of coast redwoods have been found from the south-western United States to the Arctic and occur in Britain, but the living tree is now native only to parts of the North American Pacific coast. It was first recorded in 1769, but was not described botanically until 1823, and was introduced to Britain 20 years later. It is grown in Britain mainly for its decorative value, rather than for its light, reddish-brown timber.

Some Californian coast redwoods are more than 2,500 years old, though most are less than half that age. In their native land they grow to heights of 360 ft (110 m) and more, but in Britain they are generally much smaller.

Location

Date

Habitat

Sketches

Needles are broader than those of the swamp cypress. [Actual size]

Sparse branches sweep upwards, producing a narrow, conical tree, up to 65 ft (20 m) tall. It sheds its branchlets and needles in autumn.

Needles turn russet-brown from the tips before falling in the autumn.

Branchlets appear opposite each other in pairs. The twig is greenish and the cones are green, globe-shaped or cylindrical, on long stalks.

Dawn redwood *Metasequoia glyptostroboides*

Until 1941 the dawn redwood, or water fir, was known to scientists only from its fossilised remains, and was believed to have been extinct since the Pliocene era, which ended about 2 million years ago. Then botanists in China found more than 100 large specimens growing in Hupeh province, where they had escaped the attention of the European plant-hunters of the 19th century. Later, many more dawn redwoods were discovered in the same region.

Through the efforts of the Arnold Arboretum in the United States, seeds were collected from Hupeh and distributed to tree collections in North America and Europe. It was discovered that the dawn redwood can be reproduced easily from cuttings and it is now widely planted in Britain, except for Scotland where the climate is too cool for it to grow well.

Because the tree is a recent introduction, little is known about the properties of its timber and few specimens are yet old enough to bear flowers and cones. It is one of the few cone-bearing trees that sheds its needles in the autumn. The buds of the dawn redwood are unique, appearing below the branches instead of in the axils above.

Location	Sketches
Date	
Habitat	

Branchlets are alternate, and fall in autumn with the needles. The twig is reddish, and the needles, which do not appear until June, are smaller and finer than those of the dawn redwood.

Female flowers

Female flowers are small and green; male flowers lengthen to form yellow catkins in April.

Male flowers

Green at first, the globe-shaped cone turns purple in autumn before its scales open to release their seeds.

The triangular outline is distinctive. Air-roots, or pneumatophores, often rise from the surrounding soil: these help breathing in waterlogged conditions when the soil lacks oxygen. The tree grows to 65 ft (20 m).

SITES GUIDE

The damp-loving Swamp Cypress needs warm summers to flourish, so it is seldom seen in northern Britain.

It may be seen at sites numbers: 2, 9-11, 14, 16, 24, 26-28, 30, 31, 42, 47, 50.

Swamp cypress *Taxodium distichum*

Addicts of old Hollywood films would recognise the swamp cypress on its home ground – the brackish or freshwater swamps of the south–east United States – its fallen trunks festooned with Spanish moss and its weird 'air-roots' sprouting from the mud. In prehistoric times the tree grew in Britain, for traces have been found in rocks near Bournemouth. It was introduced in 1640 by John Tradescant, and its spectacular autumn colouring made it a favourite for planting beside lakes.

In the sluggish waters of its native habitat oxygen is limited. The swamp cypress thrives there because, like the mangrove, it increases the oxygen supply by pushing up air-roots, or pneumatophores, from its root system. These are hollow structures that grow up to 10 ft (3 m) above the ground in the wild. The most usual height is 3 ft (1 m), though where adequate oxygen is available in the soil, the air-roots do not appear at all. The tree has another habit uncommon in conifers: it sheds its needles in winter, hence its alternative name of 'bald cypress'.

The wood resists damp and insects, and does not shrink; it is also soft and easily worked. These qualities make it popular for window frames and for garden buildings.

Location

Date

Habitat

Sketches

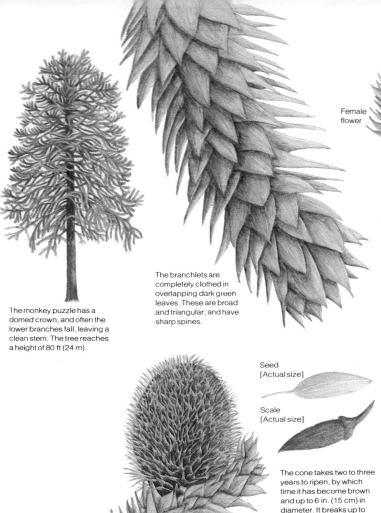

The monkey puzzle has a domed crown, and often the lower branches fall, leaving a clean stem. The tree reaches a height of 80 ft (24 m).

The branchlets are completely clothed in overlapping dark green leaves. These are broad and triangular, and have sharp spines.

Female flower

Male flowers

Male and female flowers grow on separate trees. The female flowers appear singly, the male flowers in groups.

SITES GUIDE

The Monkey Puzzle became popular in Victorian times and is still a feature of many parks and suburban gardens.

It may be seen at sites numbers: 2, 3, 7, 13, 21, 30, 37, 42, 44, 45, 47, 54.

Seed
[Actual size]

Scale
[Actual size]

The cone takes two to three years to ripen, by which time it has become brown and up to 6 in. (15 cm) in diameter. It breaks up to release seeds and scales.

Monkey puzzle *Araucaria araucana*

The monkey puzzle, or Chile pine, became known to Europeans in the 17th century because the Spaniards needed timber to build and repair their ships while they were exploiting the treasures of South America. Its discoverer was an explorer named Don Francisco Dendariarena, whom the Spanish government sent to South America specifically charged with the mission of finding a source of strong but easily worked timber.

The tree's scientific name is derived from the Araucanian Indians, who inhabited the area of southern Argentina and Chile in which it was found. The traditional explanation of the common name is that the task of climbing the tree, with its sharp, close-set leaves, would puzzle even a monkey.

The seeds of the monkey puzzle were eaten, fresh or boiled, by the Araucanian Indians. The tree was introduced to Britain in 1795 by Archibald Menzies, who saved the edible seeds served to him as a dessert and planted them on board the ship *Discovery* on which he was travelling as a botanist. The trees seldom live longer than 100 years, so no specimens of the original plantings survive today. The timber of trees grown in Britain is too knotty to be of commercial use.

Location

Date

Habitat

Sketches

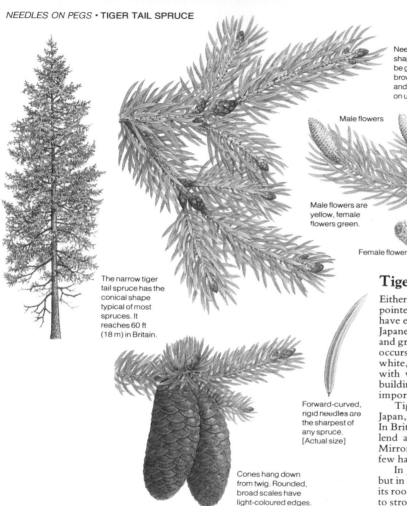

Needles are sickle-shaped and too sharp to be grasped. Chestnut-brown bud scales persist and are seen as lumps on underside of shoot.

Male flowers

Male flowers are yellow, female flowers green.

Female flower

The narrow tiger tail spruce has the conical shape typical of most spruces. It reaches 60 ft (18 m) in Britain.

Forward-curved, rigid needles are the sharpest of any spruce. [Actual size]

Cones hang down from twig. Rounded, broad scales have light-coloured edges.

SITES GUIDE

Prickly foliage makes the Tiger Tail Spruce unsuitable for all but the largest gardens and tree collections.

It may be seen at sites numbers: 10, 12, 37, 45.

Tiger tail spruce *Picea polita*

Either the long, dangling branches on older trees or the sharp-pointed needles, which are painful to grasp even lightly, may have earned this spruce its name of tiger tail – *torano-wo-nomi* in Japanese. It comes from the cool, temperate regions of Japan, and grows wild only in inaccessible valleys, where it sometimes occurs in mixed clumps with hardwoods. Its timber is soft and white, giving it the alternative name of white fir which it shares with various other species. The wood is sometimes used for building or for pulp, but is generally of little commercial importance, because of the remoteness of its growing areas.

Tiger tail spruces are widely planted as ornamental trees in Japan, often to provide shade for Shinto and Buddhist temples. In Britain, where they were introduced in the 19th century, they lend an exotic eastern appearance to many tree collections. Mirroring the Japanese custom of siting them in holy places, a few have been planted in English churchyards.

In Japan, the tiger tail spruce grows to about 130 ft (40 m), but in Britain few have attained half that height. Like all spruces, its root system is shallow and it is easily blown down if exposed to strong winds.

Location

Date

Habitat

Sketches

Female flowers

Male flowers

Male and female flowers are crimson when unripe, but turn yellow when they ripen, before shedding pollen.

Needles have blunt tips and are greenish on top and whitish beneath. They point outwards at the side of the shoot and forwards at the end. The twig is reddish.

Bluish foliage, reaching to the ground, and a very narrow crown distinguish the Serbian spruce; it grows to about 85 ft (26 m).

Scale [Actual size]

The cones taper to a point; they are bluish at first, turning rich brown with rounded scales.

SITES GUIDE

The Serbian Spruce, a popular choice for parks and gardens, is also sometimes found in small plantations.

It may be seen at sites numbers: 6, 13, 14, 47.

Serbian spruce *Picea omorika*

The only place where the Serbian spruce survived the advance and ravages of the sheets of ice during the Ice Age was a valley in Yugoslavia. There it clung tenaciously to the limestone mountains, as it does to this day. Competition from other species is small, and the cool, moist conditions favour its growth. In 1889 the tree was introduced to Britain.

Since the tree is so hardy, it had been hoped that the Serbian spruce could be grown as a forest tree, but it grew too slowly. Instead, with its crown like a spire, it is often grown as a striking ornamental conifer. It grows well on chalky soils, but is very adaptable and will grow equally well on a wide range of soils.

The Serbian spruce is less damaged by frost than either the Norway or Sitka spruces, because it comes into leaf later in the year when the risk of frost is reduced. It grows slowly but surely, stands firm against strong winds, tolerates pollution and is not affected by insect pests. There are a number of garden cultivars and there exists a hybrid with the fast-growing Sitka spruce. Hopes that this would combine hardiness with fast growth have been disappointed; it still grows too slowly to provide a good source of commercial timber.

Location

Date

Habitat

Sketches

The glossy, dark green needles, which have rounded ends, are shorter than those of any other spruce. Immature cones are pale green.

Male flowers

This narrow, conical tree has dense branches and foliage. It grows to about 130 ft (40 m). A dwarf form is often grown in rockeries.

Male flowers are dark red at first, turning yellow when they ripen and shed their pollen.

Dwarf form

Cones are narrow and slightly curved, tapering at both ends.

SITES GUIDE

The Oriental Spruce, from the Caucasus mountains of Turkey, is common throughout Britain in large gardens.

It may be seen at sites numbers: 2, 10, 12-14, 22, 26, 27, 37, 38, 43.

Oriental spruce *Picea orientalis*

In its homelands in the Caucasus and Eastern Europe the oriental spruce grows at heights of up to 7,000 ft (2,130 m). In Britain, where it has been grown since 1839, the tree is found most frequently in parks and gardens, where it is grown in a number of forms. Its cultivars include the particularly attractive 'Pendula', with weeping branches, and 'Aurea' which, as a dwarf tree, is spectacular in the spring.

Very small needles, which lie close to the stem and have blunt rather than pointed tips, distinguish oriental spruce from the similar and more widely grown Norway spruce. The tree grows slowly at first but, once established, grows rapidly in height and girth. When grown in forest plantations in Britain it has produced high yields of timber similar to that of the Norway spruce.

Because sites where the oriental spruce would grow well are already occupied by the Norway spruce, the tree has not been planted extensively for timber. But it is hardy, adaptable, grows in a wide range of conditions and is believed to be less susceptible to attack by insects than the Norway spruce. So it may one day find a place in Britain's countryside as well as in gardens.

Location	Sketches
Date	
Habitat	

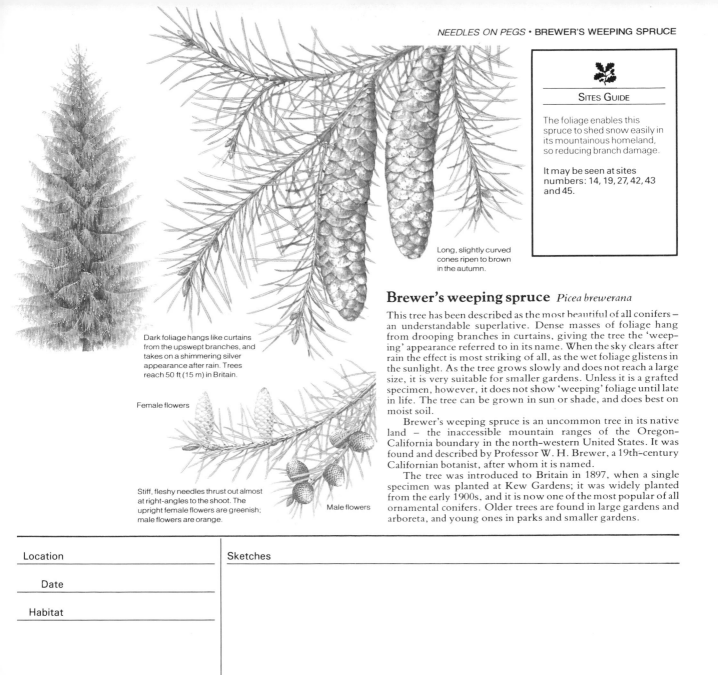

Long, slightly curved cones ripen to brown in the autumn.

Dark foliage hangs like curtains from the upswept branches, and takes on a shimmering silver appearance after rain. Trees reach 50 ft (15 m) in Britain.

Female flowers

Stiff, fleshy needles thrust out almost at right-angles to the shoot. The upright female flowers are greenish; male flowers are orange.

Male flowers

Brewer's weeping spruce *Picea brewerana*

This tree has been described as the most beautiful of all conifers – an understandable superlative. Dense masses of foliage hang from drooping branches in curtains, giving the tree the 'weeping' appearance referred to in its name. When the sky clears after rain the effect is most striking of all, as the wet foliage glistens in the sunlight. As the tree grows slowly and does not reach a large size, it is very suitable for smaller gardens. Unless it is a grafted specimen, however, it does not show 'weeping' foliage until late in life. The tree can be grown in sun or shade, and does best on moist soil.

Brewer's weeping spruce is an uncommon tree in its native land – the inaccessible mountain ranges of the Oregon-California boundary in the north-western United States. It was found and described by Professor W. H. Brewer, a 19th-century Californian botanist, after whom it is named.

The tree was introduced to Britain in 1897, when a single specimen was planted at Kew Gardens; it was widely planted from the early 1900s, and it is now one of the most popular of all ornamental conifers. Older trees are found in large gardens and arboreta, and young ones in parks and smaller gardens.

Location

Date

Habitat

Sketches

Male flowers

Female cone

Long, pointed needles, shiny green on both sides, curve forwards. Buds are large and red-brown. Flowers open in May.

Hanging foliage gives the same weeping appearance as Brewer's spruce, but the curtain effect is less marked. Trees usually grow to about 120 ft (36 m).

The cone ripens to a shiny brown.

The young cone is light green with a long, pointed outline. Its scales are smoothly rounded.

SITES GUIDE

The Morinda is a spruce native to the Himalayas, from Afghanistan to Nepal. It is also called West Himalayan Spruce.

It may be seen at sites numbers: 1, 4, 10, 27, 43.

Morinda *Picea smithiana*

The drops of resin found on the young cones of this tall, handsome conifer gave rise to its native name of morinda, a Himalayan word meaning 'the honey of flowers'. Among its alternative names is weeping fir, descriptive of its characteristic drooping branches. Their shape is helpful in allowing the morinda to shed the great weight of snow that it has to bear, for it grows in the Himalayas up to a height of 12,000 ft (3,700 m). The wood is soft and white, rather like Norway spruce.

The morinda was introduced to Britain in 1818, the Smith referred to in its botanical name being the gardener of Hopetoun House, Lothian, who first grew it in Scotland. It makes a distinguished tree in big parks and gardens, where it has ample space to grow; and although the young tree is prone to damage by spring frosts, it is hardy once established and grows rapidly. It can withstand moderate shade and grows best in moist soils.

The only other spruce with which the morinda might be confused is Brewer's spruce, a native of the Oregon and California mountains with long, drooping branches. The morinda, however, has round and not flat needles like those of Brewer's spruce, and its shoots are hairless.

Location	Sketches
Date	
Habitat	

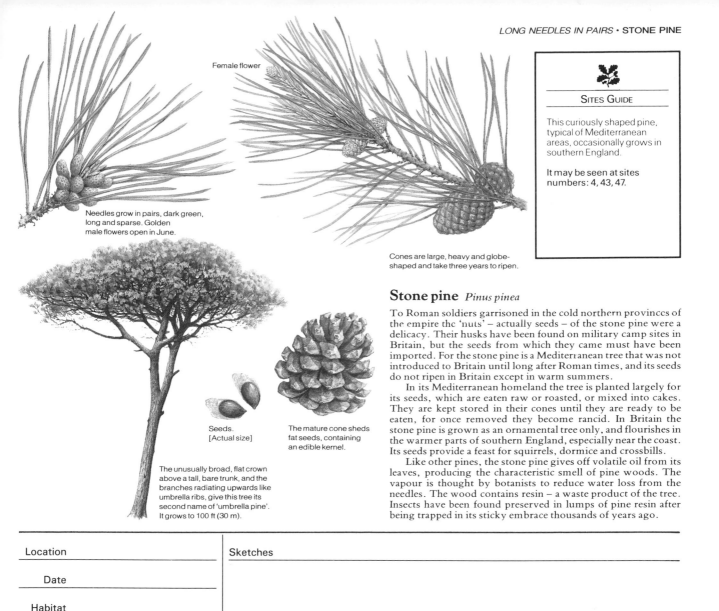

Female flower

Needles grow in pairs, dark green, long and sparse. Golden male flowers open in June.

Cones are large, heavy and globe-shaped and take three years to ripen.

SITES GUIDE

This curiously shaped pine, typical of Mediterranean areas, occasionally grows in southern England.

It may be seen at sites numbers: 4, 43, 47.

Seeds.
[Actual size]

The mature cone sheds fat seeds, containing an edible kernel.

The unusually broad, flat crown above a tall, bare trunk, and the branches radiating upwards like umbrella ribs, give this tree its second name of 'umbrella pine'. It grows to 100 ft (30 m).

Stone pine *Pinus pinea*

To Roman soldiers garrisoned in the cold northern provinces of the empire the 'nuts' – actually seeds – of the stone pine were a delicacy. Their husks have been found on military camp sites in Britain, but the seeds from which they came must have been imported. For the stone pine is a Mediterranean tree that was not introduced to Britain until long after Roman times, and its seeds do not ripen in Britain except in warm summers.

In its Mediterranean homeland the tree is planted largely for its seeds, which are eaten raw or roasted, or mixed into cakes. They are kept stored in their cones until they are ready to be eaten, for once removed they become rancid. In Britain the stone pine is grown as an ornamental tree only, and flourishes in the warmer parts of southern England, especially near the coast. Its seeds provide a feast for squirrels, dormice and crossbills.

Like other pines, the stone pine gives off volatile oil from its leaves, producing the characteristic smell of pine woods. The vapour is thought by botanists to reduce water loss from the needles. The wood contains resin – a waste product of the tree. Insects have been found preserved in lumps of pine resin after being trapped in its sticky embrace thousands of years ago.

Location

Date

Habitat

Sketches

Upper branches are ascending, but lower branches droop downwards. The tree reaches 105 ft (32 m) in height.

Mature cones have a sharp prickle or spine, curving slightly downward, on their scales. The cones are egg-shaped and up to 4 in. (10 cm) long.

Long, dark green or grey needles are slender, sharp-tipped and bunched together in groups of three. Male flowers are purple. Dull red female flowers appear at the tips of the shoots.

Jeffrey's pine
Pinus jeffreyi

Jeffrey's pine, also from western North America, is similar in appearance to the western yellow pine, but its needles are shorter and stiffer and its cones are much larger.

SITES GUIDE

Lofty Western Yellow Pines, widespread in western North America, have been planted as ornamental trees in Britain.

They may be seen at sites numbers: 19, 34, 43. Jeffrey's Pine may be seen at site number: 30.

Western yellow pine *Pinus ponderosa*

It was with this pine that the technique of dendrochronology, or tree–ring dating, was first developed in the western United States in 1901. Every year, trees in temperate regions add to their girth by laying down a light-coloured band of spring wood and one of darker summer wood. Their width depends on whether the year is wet, producing a broad band, or dry, when the band is narrow. If the annual ring variations are compared with those from tree remains on archaeological sites, these remains can be dated.

The wood of the tree is yellow, as its name suggests. The alternative names of big pine and bull pine indicate the size to which the tree can grow. A fourth name, heavy pine, is a further reference to the wood, which is hard compared with that of the white or soft pines. It is close-grained and easy to work, but is not used commercially in Britain.

Western yellow pine is planted in Britain as an ornamental tree, but because it reaches such a large size it can only be planted in big gardens. Like all pines it likes plenty of light, though it will stand shade better than some species. A very similar tree, *Pinus jeffreyi*, has shorter, darker and stiffer needles.

Location	Sketches
Date	
Habitat	

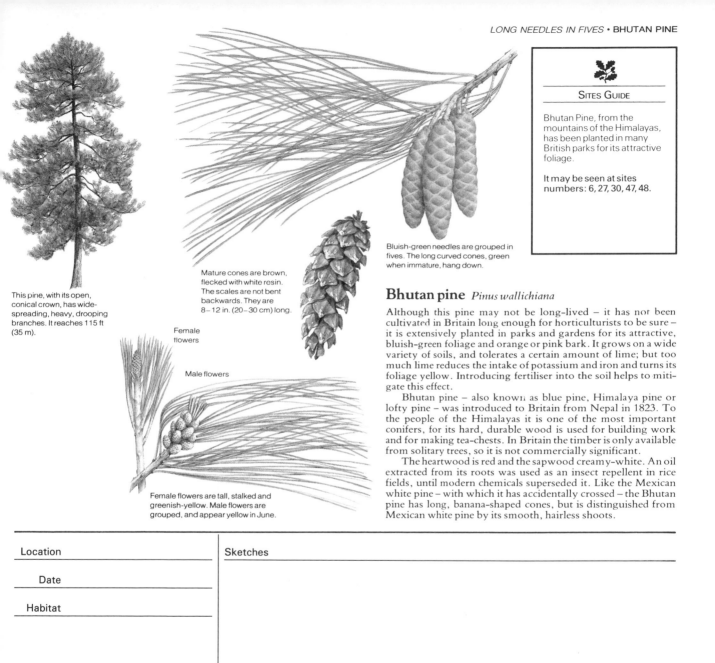

SITES GUIDE

Bhutan Pine, from the mountains of the Himalayas, has been planted in many British parks for its attractive foliage.

It may be seen at sites numbers: 6, 27, 30, 47, 48.

This pine, with its open, conical crown, has wide-spreading, heavy, drooping branches. It reaches 115 ft (35 m).

Mature cones are brown, flecked with white resin. The scales are not bent backwards. They are 8–12 in. (20–30 cm) long.

Female flowers

Male flowers

Female flowers are tall, stalked and greenish-yellow. Male flowers are grouped, and appear yellow in June.

Bluish-green needles are grouped in fives. The long curved cones, green when immature, hang down.

Bhutan pine *Pinus wallichiana*

Although this pine may not be long-lived – it has not been cultivated in Britain long enough for horticulturists to be sure – it is extensively planted in parks and gardens for its attractive, bluish-green foliage and orange or pink bark. It grows on a wide variety of soils, and tolerates a certain amount of lime; but too much lime reduces the intake of potassium and iron and turns its foliage yellow. Introducing fertiliser into the soil helps to mitigate this effect.

Bhutan pine – also known as blue pine, Himalaya pine or lofty pine – was introduced to Britain from Nepal in 1823. To the people of the Himalayas it is one of the most important conifers, for its hard, durable wood is used for building work and for making tea-chests. In Britain the timber is only available from solitary trees, so it is not commercially significant.

The heartwood is red and the sapwood creamy-white. An oil extracted from its roots was used as an insect repellent in rice fields, until modern chemicals superseded it. Like the Mexican white pine – with which it has accidentally crossed – the Bhutan pine has long, banana-shaped cones, but is distinguished from Mexican white pine by its smooth, hairless shoots.

Location	Sketches
Date	
Habitat	

The knotty trunk has short, level branches that often grow almost down to the ground. The tree can reach a height of 70 ft (22 m).

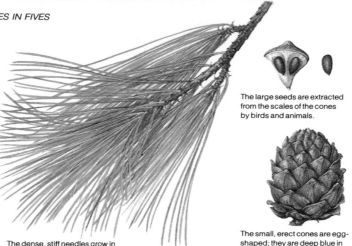

The dense, stiff needles grow in groups of five. They are shiny green on top and whitish beneath, with hairy shoots.

The large seeds are extracted from the scales of the cones by birds and animals.

The small, erect cones are egg-shaped; they are deep blue in summer, ripening to red-brown.

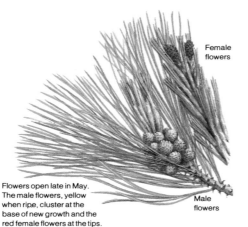

Female flowers

Male flowers

Flowers open late in May. The male flowers, yellow when ripe, cluster at the base of new growth and the red female flowers at the tips.

SITES GUIDE

Alpine in origin, the Arolla Pine adds its decorative, bushy profile to parks, large gardens and tree collections.

It may be seen at sites numbers: 22, 27, 37, 38, 48.

Arolla pine *Pinus cembra*

This small, densely branched tree, introduced to Britain in 1746 by the Duke of Argyll, grows at higher altitudes than any other European pine, and is found at 5,000–8,000 ft (1,500–2,400 m) in its native Alps and Carpathians. It grows slowly, an advantage in smaller gardens. It keeps its lower branches right down to the ground as it grows older, and its hairy young shoots are orange-brown in colour, distinguishing it from other pines with five needles, such as the Macedonian pine. These features, together with the attractive purple cones – produced when the tree is about 25 years old – make it a decorative ornamental tree for light, well-drained soils.

Unlike other pine cones the cones of Arolla pine never open naturally. The seeds are dispersed only when the cone rots on the ground or is opened by squirrels and birds seeking the seeds. As the tree does not use the wind to spread its seeds, they have no 'wings' like those of other pine seeds.

When free of knots, the soft wood of Arolla pine is easily worked and valued in its mountain homeland for decorative panelling. In the Austrian Tyrol it is used for carving small figures and animals.

Location

Date

Habitat

Sketches

Blue-green needles are slender and grow in groups of five. [Actual size]

Needles are bunched towards the ends of the twigs. The fairly large, cylindrical immature cones are bright green and hang down.

This pine can grow to 70 ft (22 m). Its dense crown is similar to that of the Arolla pine. The lower branches are often heavy but keep a symmetrical shape.

Cone is long, resinous and curved. It ripens to red-brown.

Female flowers

Male flowers

Male flowers are pale yellow; females dark red. The hairless, light green shoot distinguishes this tree from the Arolla pine.

Macedonian pine *Pinus peuce*

A native of three small areas in the Balkans, the Macedonian pine was introduced to Britain in 1864. It grows slowly and steadily, forming a very regular outline, which should make it attractive to landscape designers; but it has not been grown to any great extent outside arboreta. A few experimental forestry plantations have been established on exposed high ground in northern Britain, where the tree has shown itself able to withstand severe cold and wind.

The Macedonian pine is useful as a windbreak tree because it retains its branches right down to the ground as it grows older, the deep blue-green branches of needles forming dense foliage and an efficient barrier. The persistent branches means that the timber is knotty and of poor quality, so that the future of the tree in Britain seems to be limited to ornamental uses as an addition to parks and tree collections.

The apple-green colour of its shoots distinguishes the Macedonian pine from all other pines commonly grown in Britain. The cones are long and similar to those of the Bhutan pine, to which the tree is closely related; but they are smaller. Much resin oozes out if the bark of the tree is damaged.

Location

Date

Habitat

Sketches

The small leaves curve away from the twig. Cones, large and corky when ripe, have scales with a characteristic groove.

This narrow, conical tree, with a pointed crown, has branches that sweep down, then up at their ends. It reaches 150 ft (46 m) in Britain.

The cones, green when immature, take two years to ripen.

Female

Male

Male flowers are pale yellow in spring. Female flowers are green. Both grow at the ends of the shoots.

SITES GUIDE

The Wellingtonia, with its soft, thick, fibrous bark, can be seen in avenues and parks in Britain and in Ireland.

It may be seen at sites numbers: 2, 5, 6, 10, 12, 14, 16, 19, 22, 23, 26, 27, 30, 31, 33, 37, 39, 40, 43-47, 55.

Wellingtonia *Sequoiadendron giganteum*

Avenues of Wellingtonia were planted on many large estates in Britain soon after the tree was discovered in America in 1852. Among the most famous of these avenues is one on the Duke of Wellington's estate at Stratfield Saye in Hampshire, where this conifer was first planted in 1857. In Britain the tree was named after the 'Iron Duke', who died in the year of its discovery; but in America it is called by a variety of names reflecting its great size – among them big tree, mammoth tree and giant sequoia.

The Wellingtonia has lived up to 3,400 years in its native California. Until recently, it was thought to be the oldest-known living tree, but the bristle cone pine was found to be even longer-lived, by some 1,600 years. The Wellingtonia grows well in Britain on a wide range of soils, though its remarkably tall crown is often struck by lightning and dies at the top.

The purplish or red-brown wood is very light and brittle, so that when large trees are felled they often break up and are of little use. The thick, spongy bark is fire-resistant, as it does not contain resin. It is rich in tannins and other chemicals, and even when a fallen tree has lain on the forest floor for many years it decays hardly at all.

Location

Date

Habitat

Sketches

Male flowers

Female flowers

SITES GUIDE

This Japanese ornamental tree is common in larger gardens in rural areas, growing best in cool, damp parts of Britain and Ireland.

It may be seen at sites numbers: 1, 4, 13, 14, 16, 27, 39, 42, 43, 47-49.

Long, awl-like needles are arranged round the shoot. Male flowers are globular, brownish-yellow; females are small green rosettes.

The common garden cultivar 'Elegans' retains its juvenile juniper-like foliage throughout its life. The soft grey-green needles turn a rich bronze in autumn.

A bright green, narrowly conical crown and pale brownish-red bark distinguish the Japanese red cedar, which attains a height of 115 ft (35 m).

Round cones, with curved hooks on scales, ripen dark brown. Part of the shoot may stick out of the top.

Japanese red cedar *Cryptomeria japonica*

In its native Japan, the ornamental red cedar is often planted in gardens and along avenues near temples. It is known there by such picturesque names as 'peacock pine' and 'goddess of mercy fir'. The tree is a close relative of the Wellingtonia, which it resembles in shape and form, though it is smaller in size. It also occurs naturally in China, but it is the Japanese form – with shorter leaves – that was introduced to Britain in 1861.

Japanese red cedar grows quickly in Britain and is found in many gardens, as are its numerous cultivars, some of which retain their long, feathery, juvenile foliage for life. The tree can be coppiced, or cut down near the ground to produce new shoots, which is unusual among conifers. It withstands a lot of shade and flourishes if grown under other trees. Its dense foliage keeps out a great deal of sunlight, and so prevents the growth of weeds. The lower branches are shed early in life and produce fragrant, knot-free timber without pruning.

The timber has red heartwood and yellowish sapwood, and is strong, durable and easy to work. In Japan, it is used for building and general purposes; but in Britain it has only occasionally been planted as a forest tree.

Location

Date

Habitat

Sketches

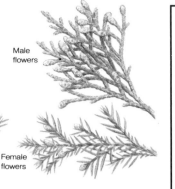

Male flowers

Female flowers

Male flowers are numerous and bright yellow; green female flowers are inconspicuous, in leaf axils.

Sites Guide

Chinese Juniper is the most commonly planted juniper in British gardens; it is also found in parks and churchyards.

It may be seen at sites numbers: 6, 13, 14, 36.

The golden foliage of the slender cultivar 'Aurea' makes it a popular ornamental tree.

A very narrow, conical, many-branched profile and an open crown characterise this juniper. It reaches a height of 60 ft (18 m).

Mature foliage consists of very small, scale-like leaves and branchlets with a spotted appearance. Juvenile leaves, ⅜ in. (1 cm) long, are awl-shaped and grow in twos and threes.

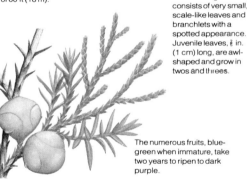

The numerous fruits, blue-green when immature, take two years to ripen to dark purple.

Chinese juniper *Juniperus chinensis*

The bluish berries of the Chinese juniper are an attractive addition to any park or garden. In order to produce the berries – which take two years to mature – the trees are best planted in groups, as the male and female flowers are on separate trees. Numerous cultivars of the Chinese juniper can be grown; some of them are different forms of the same species, while others are crosses with other species of juniper.

One of the most popular garden forms is 'Pfitzerana', a hybrid between the Chinese juniper and the savin (*Juniperus sabina*) – a European juniper grown in Britain since 1548. The spreading 'Pfitzerana' cultivar is very suitable for low ground cover. A number of blue and grey-blue forms are also available, and many retain their awl-shaped juvenile leaves for life. Another greatly admired cultivar is 'Aurea', a golden tree.

Chinese juniper and the pencil cedar are the only junipers that assume tree form; the other junipers are really shrubs. The tree and its cultivars are slow-growing and short-lived, and thrive on a wide range of soils and situations. This ornamental tree came to Britain from the Far East in 1804, and in Japan it is grown in gardens and near temples.

Location		Sketches
Date		
Habitat		

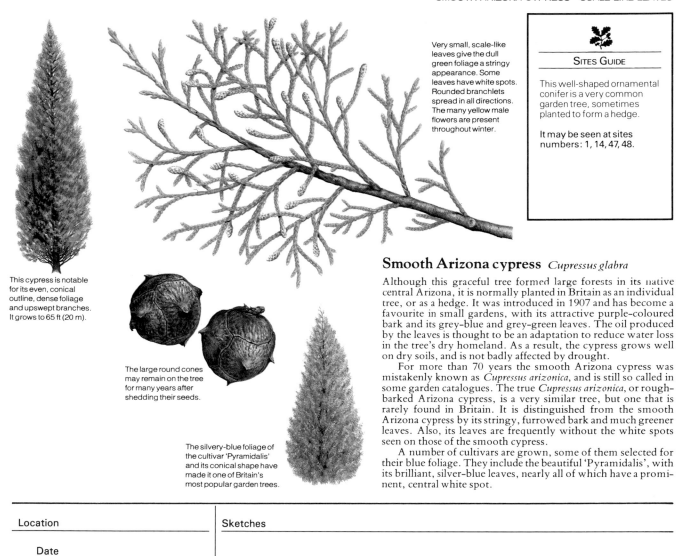

Very small, scale-like leaves give the dull green foliage a stringy appearance. Some leaves have white spots. Rounded branchlets spread in all directions. The many yellow male flowers are present throughout winter.

SITES GUIDE

This well-shaped ornamental conifer is a very common garden tree, sometimes planted to form a hedge.

It may be seen at sites numbers: 1, 14, 47, 48.

This cypress is notable for its even, conical outline, dense foliage and upswept branches. It grows to 65 ft (20 m).

The large round cones may remain on the tree for many years after shedding their seeds.

The silvery-blue foliage of the cultivar 'Pyramidalis' and its conical shape have made it one of Britain's most popular garden trees.

Smooth Arizona cypress *Cupressus glabra*

Although this graceful tree formed large forests in its native central Arizona, it is normally planted in Britain as an individual tree, or as a hedge. It was introduced in 1907 and has become a favourite in small gardens, with its attractive purple-coloured bark and its grey-blue and grey-green leaves. The oil produced by the leaves is thought to be an adaptation to reduce water loss in the tree's dry homeland. As a result, the cypress grows well on dry soils, and is not badly affected by drought.

For more than 70 years the smooth Arizona cypress was mistakenly known as *Cupressus arizonica*, and is still so called in some garden catalogues. The true *Cupressus arizonica*, or rough-barked Arizona cypress, is a very similar tree, but one that is rarely found in Britain. It is distinguished from the smooth Arizona cypress by its stringy, furrowed bark and much greener leaves. Also, its leaves are frequently without the white spots seen on those of the smooth cypress.

A number of cultivars are grown, some of them selected for their blue foliage. They include the beautiful 'Pyramidalis', with its brilliant, silver-blue leaves, nearly all of which have a prominent, central white spot.

Location

Date

Habitat

Sketches

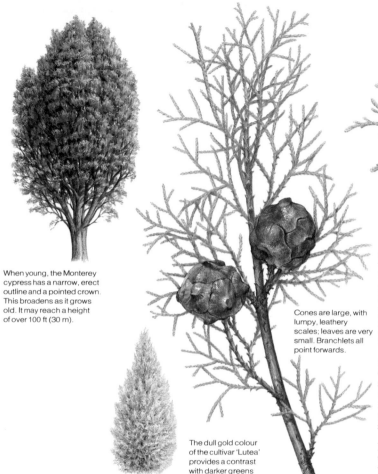

When young, the Monterey cypress has a narrow, erect outline and a pointed crown. This broadens as it grows old. It may reach a height of over 100 ft (30 m).

Cones are large, with lumpy, leathery scales; leaves are very small. Branchlets all point forwards.

The dull gold colour of the cultivar 'Lutea' provides a contrast with darker greens when planted in gardens.

The small, yellow, egg-shaped male flowers appear in late spring.

SITES GUIDE

Because it resists salt winds, this tree has probably been used more than any other for seaside planting.

It may be seen at sites numbers: 1, 8, 10, 18, 39, 43, 46-48, 54.

Monterey cypress *Cupressus macrocarpa*

When it was introduced to Britain from west California in 1838, the Monterey cypress was mainly used as a windbreak or hedge. It thrives in the south and west of Britain, where it grows on a wide range of soils. Although it is damaged and sometimes killed by frost, it is resistant to salt winds. But today its role as a hedge plant has been taken over by the faster growing Leyland cypress, a cross between this species and the Nootka cypress.

On the Monterey peninsula in California, the tree is characteristic of a narrow zone lying between the beach and the area occupied by the Monterey pine. Some of the older trees are shaped into picturesque silhouettes by the wind. Like the Monterey pine, the Monterey cypress grows well in Africa and Australasia, where it is an important timber tree. The fragrant, yellowish wood is of good quality, but it is only obtainable in small quantities in Britain.

The cypress needs to be planted out young as – like pines – it later develops a strong tap root which is easily damaged during transplanting. Container-grown plants solve this problem. The young tree has to be supported by a stake if it has much foliage, otherwise the wind may catch it and work the tree loose.

Location

Date

Habitat

Sketches

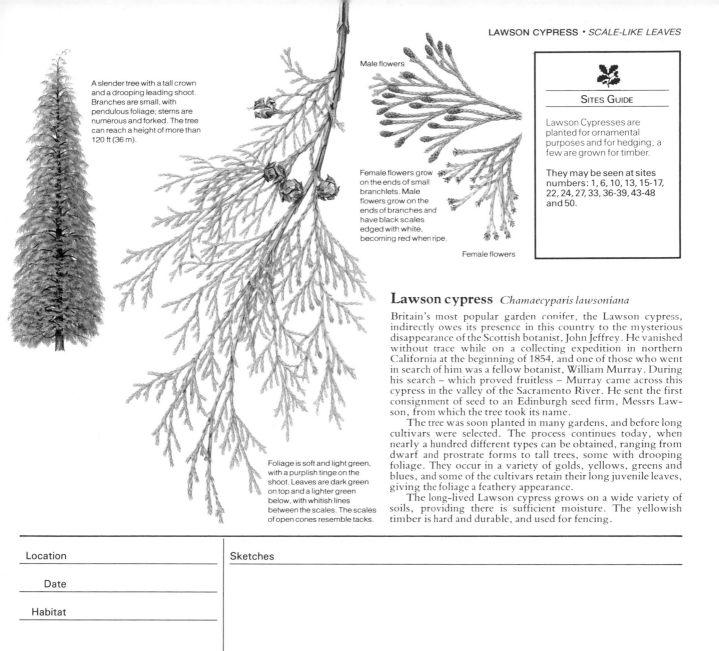

A slender tree with a tall crown and a drooping leading shoot. Branches are small, with pendulous foliage; stems are numerous and forked. The tree can reach a height of more than 120 ft (36 m).

Male flowers

Female flowers grow on the ends of small branchlets. Male flowers grow on the ends of branches and have black scales edged with white, becoming red when ripe.

Female flowers

Foliage is soft and light green, with a purplish tinge on the shoot. Leaves are dark green on top and a lighter green below, with whitish lines between the scales. The scales of open cones resemble tacks.

Sites Guide

Lawson Cypresses are planted for ornamental purposes and for hedging; a few are grown for timber.

They may be seen at sites numbers: 1, 6, 10, 13, 15-17, 22, 24, 27, 33, 36-39, 43-48 and 50.

Lawson cypress *Chamaecyparis lawsoniana*

Britain's most popular garden conifer, the Lawson cypress, indirectly owes its presence in this country to the mysterious disappearance of the Scottish botanist, John Jeffrey. He vanished without trace while on a collecting expedition in northern California at the beginning of 1854, and one of those who went in search of him was a fellow botanist, William Murray. During his search – which proved fruitless – Murray came across this cypress in the valley of the Sacramento River. He sent the first consignment of seed to an Edinburgh seed firm, Messrs Lawson, from which the tree took its name.

The tree was soon planted in many gardens, and before long cultivars were selected. The process continues today, when nearly a hundred different types can be obtained, ranging from dwarf and prostrate forms to tall trees, some with drooping foliage. They occur in a variety of golds, yellows, greens and blues, and some of the cultivars retain their long juvenile leaves, giving the foliage a feathery appearance.

The long-lived Lawson cypress grows on a wide variety of soils, providing there is sufficient moisture. The yellowish timber is hard and durable, and used for fencing.

Location

Date

Habitat

Sketches

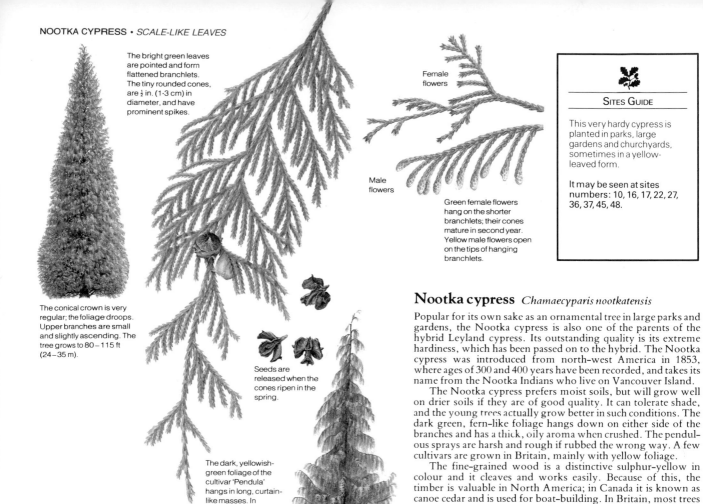

The bright green leaves are pointed and form flattened branchlets. The tiny rounded cones, are ½ in. (1·3 cm) in diameter, and have prominent spikes.

The conical crown is very regular; the foliage droops. Upper branches are small and slightly ascending. The tree grows to 80–115 ft (24–35 m).

Seeds are released when the cones ripen in the spring.

The dark, yellowish-green foliage of the cultivar 'Pendula' hangs in long, curtain-like masses. In summer the cones turn shiny blue.

Female flowers

Male flowers

Green female flowers hang on the shorter branchlets; their cones mature in second year. Yellow male flowers open on the tips of hanging branchlets.

Nootka cypress *Chamaecyparis nootkatensis*

Popular for its own sake as an ornamental tree in large parks and gardens, the Nootka cypress is also one of the parents of the hybrid Leyland cypress. Its outstanding quality is its extreme hardiness, which has been passed on to the hybrid. The Nootka cypress was introduced from north-west America in 1853, where ages of 300 and 400 years have been recorded, and takes its name from the Nootka Indians who live on Vancouver Island.

The Nootka cypress prefers moist soils, but will grow well on drier soils if they are of good quality. It can tolerate shade, and the young trees actually grow better in such conditions. The dark green, fern-like foliage hangs down on either side of the branches and has a thick, oily aroma when crushed. The pendulous sprays are harsh and rough if rubbed the wrong way. A few cultivars are grown in Britain, mainly with yellow foliage.

The fine-grained wood is a distinctive sulphur-yellow in colour and it cleaves and works easily. Because of this, the timber is valuable in North America; in Canada it is known as canoe cedar and is used for boat-building. In Britain, most trees are relatively young and the species has not been exploited commercially for its timber.

Location

Date

Habitat

Sketches

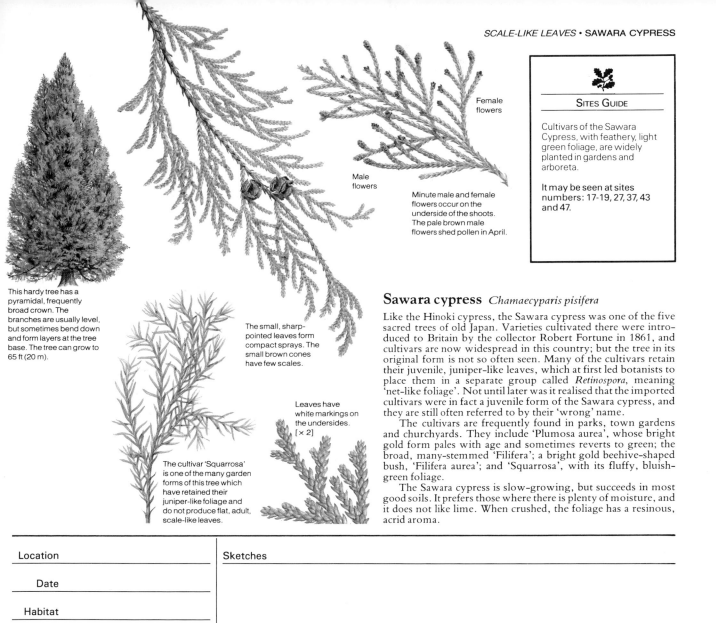

This hardy tree has a pyramidal, frequently broad crown. The branches are usually level, but sometimes bend down and form layers at the tree base. The tree can grow to 65 ft (20 m).

Female flowers

Male flowers

Minute male and female flowers occur on the underside of the shoots. The pale brown male flowers shed pollen in April.

The small, sharp-pointed leaves form compact sprays. The small brown cones have few scales.

Leaves have white markings on the undersides. [× 2]

The cultivar 'Squarrosa' is one of the many garden forms of this tree which have retained their juniper-like foliage and do not produce flat, adult, scale-like leaves.

SITES GUIDE

Cultivars of the Sawara Cypress, with feathery, light green foliage, are widely planted in gardens and arboreta.

It may be seen at sites numbers: 17-19, 27, 37, 43 and 47.

Sawara cypress *Chamaecyparis pisifera*

Like the Hinoki cypress, the Sawara cypress was one of the five sacred trees of old Japan. Varieties cultivated there were introduced to Britain by the collector Robert Fortune in 1861, and cultivars are now widespread in this country; but the tree in its original form is not so often seen. Many of the cultivars retain their juvenile, juniper-like leaves, which at first led botanists to place them in a separate group called *Retinospora*, meaning 'net-like foliage'. Not until later was it realised that the imported cultivars were in fact a juvenile form of the Sawara cypress, and they are still often referred to by their 'wrong' name.

The cultivars are frequently found in parks, town gardens and churchyards. They include 'Plumosa aurea', whose bright gold form pales with age and sometimes reverts to green; the broad, many-stemmed 'Filifera'; a bright gold beehive-shaped bush, 'Filifera aurea'; and 'Squarrosa', with its fluffy, bluish-green foliage.

The Sawara cypress is slow-growing, but succeeds in most good soils. It prefers those where there is plenty of moisture, and it does not like lime. When crushed, the foliage has a resinous, acrid aroma.

Location

Date

Habitat

Sketches

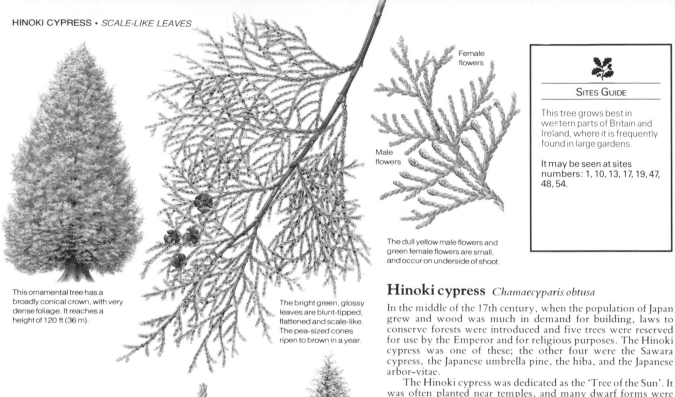

This ornamental tree has a broadly conical crown, with very dense foliage. It reaches a height of 120 ft (36 m).

The bright green, glossy leaves are blunt-tipped, flattened and scale-like. The pea-sized cones ripen to brown in a year.

Undersides of leaves have pronounced white markings.

The golden cultivar 'Crippsii' grows slowly and suits rockeries. It tolerates shade.

Female flowers

Male flowers

The dull yellow male flowers and green female flowers are small, and occur on underside of shoot.

SITES GUIDE

This tree grows best in western parts of Britain and Ireland, where it is frequently found in large gardens.

It may be seen at sites numbers: 1, 10, 13, 17, 19, 47, 48, 54.

Hinoki cypress *Chamaecyparis obtusa*

In the middle of the 17th century, when the population of Japan grew and wood was much in demand for building, laws to conserve forests were introduced and five trees were reserved for use by the Emperor and for religious purposes. The Hinoki cypress was one of these; the other four were the Sawara cypress, the Japanese umbrella pine, the hiba, and the Japanese arbor-vitae.

The Hinoki cypress was dedicated as the 'Tree of the Sun'. It was often planted near temples, and many dwarf forms were cultivated in gardens. It was introduced to Britain in 1861 by the collector J. G. Veitch, and is frequently seen in large gardens. It does well on moist soils, including those which are slightly acid. Numerous cultivars have been propagated, many of them slow-growing dwarf forms which are planted in rockeries. In eastern areas it is more often seen as the cultivar 'Crippsii', grown in small gardens and parks.

The bark resists decay and, in Japan, is used for roof shingles. The wood is white, fragrant, easily worked and durable. It has a beautiful grain and is much used in furniture-making in its native land.

Location

Date

Habitat

Sketches

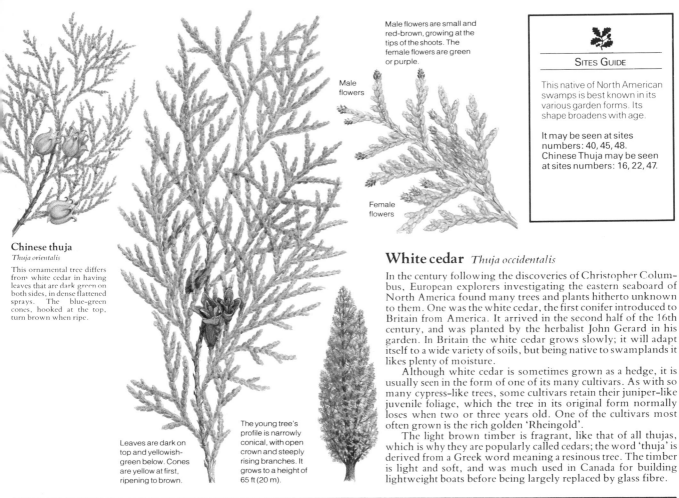

Male flowers are small and red-brown, growing at the tips of the shoots. The female flowers are green or purple.

Male flowers

Female flowers

SITES GUIDE

This native of North American swamps is best known in its various garden forms. Its shape broadens with age.

It may be seen at sites numbers: 40, 45, 48. Chinese Thuja may be seen at sites numbers: 16, 22, 47.

Chinese thuja
Thuja orientalis

This ornamental tree differs from white cedar in having leaves that are dark green on both sides, in dense flattened sprays. The blue-green cones, hooked at the top, turn brown when ripe.

Leaves are dark on top and yellowish-green below. Cones are yellow at first, ripening to brown.

The young tree's profile is narrowly conical, with open crown and steeply rising branches. It grows to a height of 65 ft (20 m).

White cedar *Thuja occidentalis*

In the century following the discoveries of Christopher Columbus, European explorers investigating the eastern seaboard of North America found many trees and plants hitherto unknown to them. One was the white cedar, the first conifer introduced to Britain from America. It arrived in the second half of the 16th century, and was planted by the herbalist John Gerard in his garden. In Britain the white cedar grows slowly; it will adapt itself to a wide variety of soils, but being native to swamplands it likes plenty of moisture.

Although white cedar is sometimes grown as a hedge, it is usually seen in the form of one of its many cultivars. As with so many cypress-like trees, some cultivars retain their juniper-like juvenile foliage, which the tree in its original form normally loses when two or three years old. One of the cultivars most often grown is the rich golden 'Rheingold'.

The light brown timber is fragrant, like that of all thujas, which is why they are popularly called cedars; the word 'thuja' is derived from a Greek word meaning a resinous tree. The timber is light and soft, and was much used in Canada for building lightweight boats before being largely replaced by glass fibre.

Location

Date

Habitat

Sketches

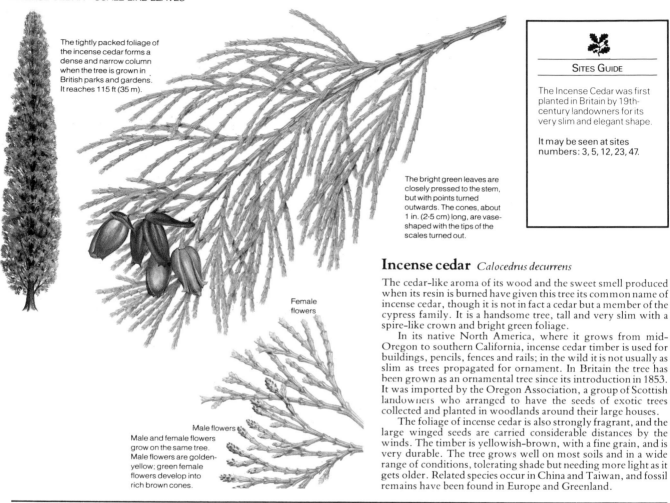

The tightly packed foliage of the incense cedar forms a dense and narrow column when the tree is grown in British parks and gardens. It reaches 115 ft (35 m).

The bright green leaves are closely pressed to the stem, but with points turned outwards. The cones, about 1 in. (2·5 cm) long, are vase-shaped with the tips of the scales turned out.

Female flowers

Male flowers

Male and female flowers grow on the same tree. Male flowers are golden-yellow; green female flowers develop into rich brown cones.

SITES GUIDE

The Incense Cedar was first planted in Britain by 19th-century landowners for its very slim and elegant shape.

It may be seen at sites numbers: 3, 5, 12, 23, 47.

Incense cedar *Calocedrus decurrens*

The cedar-like aroma of its wood and the sweet smell produced when its resin is burned have given this tree its common name of incense cedar, though it is not in fact a cedar but a member of the cypress family. It is a handsome tree, tall and very slim with a spire-like crown and bright green foliage.

In its native North America, where it grows from mid-Oregon to southern California, incense cedar timber is used for buildings, pencils, fences and rails; in the wild it is not usually as slim as trees propagated for ornament. In Britain the tree has been grown as an ornamental tree since its introduction in 1853. It was imported by the Oregon Association, a group of Scottish landowners who arranged to have the seeds of exotic trees collected and planted in woodlands around their large houses.

The foliage of incense cedar is also strongly fragrant, and the large winged seeds are carried considerable distances by the winds. The timber is yellowish-brown, with a fine grain, and is very durable. The tree grows well on most soils and in a wide range of conditions, tolerating shade but needing more light as it gets older. Related species occur in China and Taiwan, and fossil remains have been found in Europe and Greenland.

Location

Date

Habitat

Sketches

The cones, oval when closed, have few scales, each with a protuberance near its tip. They open widely to release seed. The cones are about ⅝ in. (1·6 cm) in length.

The shiny leaves have the artificial look of plastic. They have conspicuous broad white patches with a narrow green border on the undersides.

Male flowers

The green male flowers grow at the tips of branchlets. Female flowers are blue-grey and ripen to woody, oval cones.

Female flowers

The cylindrical, regularly shaped hiba is densely clothed with foliage. The tree grows 50–65 ft (15–20 m).

Hiba *Thujopsis dolabrata*

The hiba's species name of *dolabrata* – from the Latin *dolabra*, 'hatchet' – refers to the shape of its scale-like leaves, which are thought to resemble an axe-head. They are a shiny bright green, with undersides boldly marked in white, and so perfect that they seem almost artificial. Because of the continuous luxuriance of its foliage, the hiba is one of a group of trees sometimes known as *Arbor vitae*, 'tree of life'; the others are the closely related thujas.

The timber is used for building in Japan, as it is light but strong, easy to work and durable. The hiba was one of the five sacred trees of old Japan, preserved for use by the royal family and in religious practice. It was introduced to Britain in 1853, in its southern and somewhat shrubby form. The first plant to be introduced died, but others arrived in 1859 and 1861.

In Britain, the hiba is seen purely as an ornamental tree, which thrives on soils that are not lime-rich. When trees are grown in open surroundings, the branches often touch the ground and will sometimes take root. The cone scales each bear three to five seeds, unlike the thujas which have only two seeds to each scale.

Location	Sketches
Date	
Habitat	

Inverness □

44 ●

43 ● □ Aberdeen
42 ●

41 ●

Glasgow □ □ Edinburgh

40 ●

39 ●

37 ●
36 ●

38 ● □ Newcastle-upon-Tyne

Lough Neagh

46
Belfast □ ●
45 ●
47 ●

Aire **35** ●

34 ●
Leeds □ □ Kingston upon Hull

Liverpool □ □ Manchester
27 ● **28** ●

Dublin □ **30** ●
54 ● **18** □ **19** **29** ●
53 ● Bangor □

Shannon **55** ● **20** ● **31** ●

26 ● **33** ●
17 ● **25** ● **32** ●
Norwich □

24 ●
23 ● □ Birmingham
Gt Ouse

Suir

50 ●
51 ● *Blackwater*
Cork □ □ **49** **52** ●
48 ●

Severn
Thames **22** ●

Cardiff □ □ Bristol **21** ● **16** ● London □
10 ●

11 ● **15** ●
7 ● **13** ●
6 ● **9** ● Southampton
8 ● □ **12** ● **14** ●
Exeter □ **5** ●

3 ●
2 ● **4** ●
Truro □
1 ●

0   50
MILES

The Sites

A descriptive gazetteer of places around Britain to see the ornamental trees on pages 12-95.

Order

The sites are featured in a special order, designed for ease of reference. They follow each other in an order determined by the Ordnance Survey's grid reference system, which works from west to east, and from south to north. The first sites described are those in Cornwall, in other words those furthest west and furthest south; the last sites described on mainland Britain are in north-east Scotland; Ulster and the Republic of Ireland are listed separately at the end.

For additional ease of reference, the sites are however grouped in regions and counties, and this framework takes precedence over the order required by the grid system; so that for example, all the sites in Wales, from south to north, are listed together; then the list continues, starting afresh with the south-west corner of the Midlands, ie Gloucestershire.

Location of sites

Each site is described in terms of access from a nearby major road or town, or other major landmark. The number of the Ordnance Survey Landranger sheet (scale 1:50 000) on which the site occurs is also given, together with a grid reference number for exact and speedy location of the site on the map. (Full directions on how to read a numerical grid reference are given on all Landranger sheets.) A six-figure grid reference number is accurate to the nearest hundred metres and these are given where possible; however, it is sometimes more appropriate to quote a four-figure grid reference, accurate to the nearest kilometre, when a large area is in question.

Tree names in bold type

Tree names in bold are those which are featured in the identification section, pages 12-95.

Botanical terms

A glossary explaining botanical terms is on page 125.

KEY TO MAP
1 Trelissick
2 Lanhydrock
3 Cotehele
4 Saltram
5 Killerton
6 Knighthayes Court
7 Arlington Court
8 Montacute
9 Lacock Abbey
10 Stourhead
11 The Vyne
12 Petworth
13 Nymans Garden
14 Sheffield Park Garden
15 Winkworth Arboretum
16 Cliveden
17 Powis Castle
18 Plas Newydd
19 Bodnant Garden

20 Chirk Castle
21 Greys Court
22 Waddesdon Manor
23 Croft Castle
24 Dudmaston
25 Attingham Park
26 Shugborough
27 Tatton Park
28 Dunham Massey
29 Hardwick Hall
30 Clumber Park
31 Belton
32 Blickling Hall
33 Felbrigg Hall
34 Beningbrough Hall
35 Studley Royal
36 Wallington
37 Cragside
38 Threave Garden
39 Culzean

40 Brodick Castle
41 Branklyn Garden
42 Crathes
43 Drum Castle
44 Haddo House
45 Rowallane
46 Mount Stewart
47 Castle Ward
48 Ilnacullin
49 Fota Estate
50 Annes Grove Gardens
51 Muckross Gardens
52 John F. Kennedy Memorial Arboretum
53 Mount Usher Gardens
54 Powerscourt Gardens
55 Birr Castle

THE SOUTH WEST

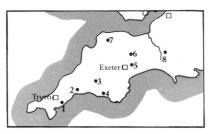

CORNWALL

1 Trelissick

LOCATION Trelissick is four miles (6.5 km) south of Truro, on both sides of the B3289 above King Harry Ferry; *Landranger Sheet 204, SW837396;* OPEN (garden only) Mar to end-Oct: Mon to Sat including Good Friday 11-6, Sun 1-6 or sunset if earlier; woodland walk also open Nov to end-Mar; ADMISSION £1.50, children £0.75.

Situated on land sloping eastwards, this garden is on each side of a valley, bisected by the B3289. To the north of the road (crossed by bridge) is a young arboretum called the Carcadden, while the part to the south comprises a woodland garden, lawns, shrub borders and a fig garden. It is a diverse garden with low duplication of tree species, so there is much more to be seen than can be listed here. The majority of the woody ornamentals are less than 50 years old; however most of the clumps of trees in the park, and the conifers in the garden, date from the mid-19th C, when the Gilbert family had them planted.

Best time of year
Appealing at all seasons; although the autumn colour is not as spectacular as in drier locations, the combination of **maple**, oxydendrum, **Persian Ironwood** and **Sweet Gum** makes a marvellous tableau in October.

Other highlights
Ninety-foot (30-m) **Japanese Red Cedar** and sycamore 'Prinz Handjery' on the main lawn; **Holm Oak, plane, deodar** and **Atlas Cedar;** also a lovely **Japanese** flowering **Cherry** with double white flowers, which grows by the house. This is one of the forerunners of the many cultivated **cherries** found scattered throughout the garden.

Most of the **magnolias,** and some attractive holly cultivars, can be found in the Carcadden, where they have been placed against a background of conifers: look for **Lawson, Hinoki** and **Monterey Cypress,** also **Smooth Japanese** and Norway **Maple.**

Other trees of interest include the semi-pendulous morinda, or West Himalayan Spruce; **hiba, Smooth Arizona Cypress;** stately eucryphia; and leaden-green **Cider Gum.** There are nine fig cultivars in the fig garden. The False Beech (*Nothofagus fusca*) in the valley side of the Carcadden is, at 70 ft (21 m), one of the tallest on record. The old leaves of this evergreen from New Zealand have the peculiar habit of turning red in spring before falling.

2 Lanhydrock

LOCATION Two-and-a-half miles (4 km) south of Bodmin on the road to Lostwithiel (B3268); *Landranger Sheet 200, SX085636;* OPEN Apr to end-Oct: every day including Good Fri and bank holidays 11-6. Nov to end-Mar: garden only open every day during daylight hours; ADMISSION (garden and grounds only) £1.50, children £0.75.

This estate overlooks the valley of the River Fowey; the garden is set on a hillside facing north-east above the house and park and is flanked by woodland, which acts as a shelter belt. Although the garden has its roots in the Victorian age, its collection is young with many of the plants having been added during the last 50 years: well worth visiting as an example of early 20th C taste.

Best time of year
Spring: main speciality is **magnolia.** Depending on the weather, the first **magnolia** displays can start as early as the second week in March and continue through to September. Some specimens have reached over 60 ft (18 m) in height, notably *M. campbellii* and *M. × veitchii,* and there is a marvellous **magnolia** tunnel constructed of *M. × soulangiana* 'Lennei'.

Other highlights
A repeated theme throughout the garden is Irish yew, one specimen reaching 50 ft (15 m) in height. In front of the house are annually-clipped Irish yews – an unusual choice for topiary because it can quickly grow out of shape. Other prominent trees are: **Smooth Japanese Maple, Silver Maple, Indian Bean Tree** and **Tulip Tree** from North America; **Foxglove Tree** and **Tree of**

Heaven from China; Purple Beech (planted by William Gladstone); **Black Walnut** and **Manna Ash.** Late-summer displays are enhanced by eucryphia while variegated forms of holly give colour to the shady western part of the gardens.

Apart from a few notable exceptions, such as **Swamp Cypress,** conifers are of small importance in the garden itself. However, Station Drive, in the valley, is totally coniferous and contains many exotic trees, such as **Oriental Spruce,** a very tall **hiba, Caucasian Fir, Noble Fir, Monkey Puzzle** and **wellingtonia,** as does the Great Wood.

3 Cotehele

LOCATION **Eight miles (13 km) south-west of Tavistock, off the A390;** *Landranger Sheet 201, SX-422685;* OPEN **(garden only) Apr to end-Oct: every day 11-6. Nov to end- Mar: during daylight hours;** ADMISSION **(garden and mill only) £1.50, children £0.75.**

Cotehele is a remarkably diverse garden of intimate and unpretentious character set on the Cornish bank of the River Tamar. The climate is generally mild and the place gives the feeling that conditions are different here from anywhere else in the region. The garden has been developed over the centuries, although its present design mostly dates from the mid-19th C. An arboretum was recently established in Nellson's Piece, north-east of the house. The grounds divide into two essentially different areas: the upper garden area around the house, and the valley garden.

Trees tend not be duplicated between the two areas.

Best time of year
Small flowering trees such as spring-flowering **magnolia** are a speciality, but recent planting has been designed to prolong the season of display into and through the summer. Autumn colour is a subsidiary feature, provided by, amongst others, **Katsura Tree, Persian Ironwood** and cultivars of Japanese Maple.

Other highlights
Cork Oak has always been a speciality at Cotehele: it grows better here than anywhere else in the country, although existing ones at present are small.

The pond in the upper garden is graced by numerous exotics such as **Tree of Heaven** from China and **Tulip Tree** and Honey Locust from North America. The largest is the yellow-stemmed, autumn-colouring 'Jaspidea' Ash. Nearby are some prolific flowering forms of **Japanese** cultivated **Cherry.** Other exotics of interest in the upper garden are an ancient **Judas Tree,** a red-flowered form of Pagoda Tree and an exceptionally rare 'Laciniata' Walnut (behind the barn).

Conifers are a relatively insignificant feature; however, tall specimens in the valley especially **Common Silver Fir** are some of the most prominent trees in the entire garden. Not so noticeable are **Monkey Puzzle,** Western Hemlock and, near the head of the valley, **Incense Cedar.** On the north side of the valley, **Dawn Redwood** and Maidenhair Fern, both from China, contribute to the autumn colour. *Acer* is represented

by 22 taxa including **Snake Bark** and **Silver Maple** in the valley garden. The purple-leaved **Smooth Japanese Maples** make a satisfying visual link with Copper Beech. Other notable exotics in the valley garden include a large American **Red Oak;** a recently planted **Handkerchief Tree;** 'Wateriana' holly with its rich gold-bordered leaves and several Chusan Palms.

DEVON

4 Saltram

LOCATION **Two miles (3 km) west of Plympton between the A38 and the A379;** *Landranger Sheet 201, SX-520557;* OPEN **(garden only) Apr to end-Oct: every day 11-6. Nov to end- Mar: every day during daylight hours;** ADMISSION **(garden only) £1.**

Saltram's garden dates from 1770, but it was substantially altered to give its present design in the 19th C by the 3rd Earl of Morley. Many of the new trees came from Westonbirt Arboretum after the Earl married Margaret Holford, the daughter of R.S. Holford of Westonbirt. A unique feature is the long avenue of **limes** within the garden itself.

Best time of year
Spring for the **magnolias, Katsura Tree** and **lime** avenue; autumn for *Acer,* beech and **Katsura Tree.**

Other highlights
Saltram was renowned for its elm trees until Dutch elm disease took its toll in

1975. Since then there has been large-scale replanting in the park with beech, *Acer* and ash in particular. Prominent species in the garden include **Holm Oak, Coast Redwood** and Monterey Pine, one 120 ft (36 m) high.

On the East Lawn are **Tulip Trees** and a mass of golden yew; but the main garden is to the west of the house. The various walks there are bordered by **magnolia** and specimen trees such as **Atlas Cedar** (by the Chapel Gallery), **Indian Bean Tree, Silver** pendent **Lime** and Cut-leaf Beech (at the east end of the lime avenue). Several other interesting beeches have been planted in the beech grove.

In the central glade there are some superb exotics including **Stone Pine, morinda, Japanese Red Cedar, Lucombe Oak,** Indian Horse Chestnut and **Paper-bark Maple.** Along North Path look out for Western Red Cedar, **Katsura Tree** and whitebeam; around the orange grove for **Cork Oak** and **Black Walnut.**

5 Killerton

LOCATION **Seven miles (11 km) north-east of Exeter, on the west side of the B3181 to Cullompton; the entrance is off the B3185;** *Landranger Sheet 192, SX9700;* OPEN **during daylight hours throughout the year;** ADMISSION **(garden and park only) £1.50, children £0.75.**

The great feature of this garden is a fine arboretum which offers delightful walking. It is on a lime-free hill in an otherwise limey district, with a gentle but windy climate and rich soil. John Veitch, the 19th-C nurseryman, was closely involved in planting trees here, and, even after his firm had moved to Exeter in 1932, Killerton went on taking specimens from his nursery. Gifts were also received from many other parts of the world and together these have made the garden a fascinating place.

Best time of year

Killerton is superb all year, but the **magnolias** make it particularly beautiful in spring. In autumn the Top Walk is aflame with the reds of **maple.** In winter the coloured barks of exotics (including the grey-white of **gum** and the dark brown of **wellingtonia**) stand out to great effect.

Other highlights

Cork Oaks; Caucasian Elm; **Handkerchief Tree** from China; giant conifers of dark green, blue and yellow, including **deodar** from the Himalayas and **Incense Cedar** and **Colorado White Fir** from North America. Guarding the chapel are two vast **Tulip Trees,** planted *c.*1800, and a **Lucombe Oak** with a girth of 17 ft (5 m).

6 Knighthayes Court

LOCATION **Off the A396, Bampton road 2 miles (3 km) north of Tiverton;** *Landranger Sheet 181, SS960151;* OPEN **(garden only) Apr to end-Oct: every day 11-6;** ADMISSION **(garden and grounds only) £1.50.**

The most outstanding feature of Knighthayes Court is its diversity of trees, which is reflected by the high number of taxa and the relative lack of duplication. It is a young garden, with a generous proportion of cultivars, and an arboretum, developed by Sir John and Lady Heathcoat Amory since World War II; in fact it can claim to be one of Britain's post-war gardens: the collection has immense vitality.

Best time of year

The gardens are designed to be of interest throughout the year.

Other highlights

A newly-planted collection of **willows** fills a natural circular depression across the drive, where can be found 35 taxa of *Salix,* as well as many interesting chestnuts (including one from California); **Bhutan Pine;** Norway Maple and young elms. Around the drive occur 32 taxa of **oak,** including various extremely rare ones; nearer the house are concentrated most of the 29 taxa of **rowan.**

Another major speciality of Knighthayes Court is *Acer* (67 taxa). Many species are rare, introduced from, for example, Taiwan, Japan and North America. They include cultivars or forms of Japanese Maple; **Red Maple;** Norway Maple; **Snake-bark Maple; Cappadocian Maple** and sycamore. Other collections of interest are birch, **magnolia, juniper,** flowering **cherry** and holly. Most of the **junipers** are in the dwarf conifer area in Michael's Wood, with rare specimens from Eurasia and China represented.

Cedar of Lebanon dominates the south garden and in the same area are

Atlas Cedar (including one that is the biggest specimen in Britain); a very tall **juniper** from China; False Beech *(Nothofagus)* from both New Zealand and South America; **Locust Tree** and **Lucombe Oak.**

Interesting exotics to the east of the house include a tender Mexican Fir, **Colorado White Fir, Serbian Spruce,** and cultivars of **Lawson Cypress, deodar, Cedar of Lebanon** and Grey Alder. In the park are an ancient **wellingtonia** and an immense **Turkey Oak** with the largest recorded girth in Britain.

7 Arlington Court

LOCATION Seven miles (11 km) north-east of Barnstaple on the east side of the A39; *Landranger Sheet 180, SS611405;* OPEN (garden and park only) Apr to end-Oct: every day 11-6. Nov to end-Mar: during daylight hours; ADMISSION (garden, grounds and stable only) £1.50.

Standing 600 ft (180 m) above sea-level and exposed to strong westerly gales, Arlington is not an ideal site for growing trees. However, some fine specimens have survived from the original plantings in the mid-19th C, and there are some interesting young exotics.

Best time of year
The **Tulip Trees** are usually resplendent in late July. Their autumn colours are impressive, too, as are those of the **Maidenhair Tree** in the formal garden.

Other highlights
On the edge of the front lawn stands a large **Turkey Oak,** about 100 years old. Nearby are two specimens, with variegated leaves, of a form of sycamore. Beyond, there is the oldest of the **Tulip Trees** – an interesting specimen, covered in bumps and bulges.

Above the pond are **hiba** and several young **ash** trees, including **Manna Ash;** on the terrace to the formal garden are two small **Monkey Puzzles.**

SOMERSET

8 Montacute

LOCATION About 4 miles (6.5 km) west of Yeovil on the north side of the A3088; *Landranger Sheet 183, ST499172;* OPEN (garden and park) all year every day: 12.30-6 or dusk if earlier; ADMISSION (garden and park) June to end-Sept £0.80. Oct to end-May £0.60.

Here you will find not only a formal garden but also a landscaped park. The garden seen today is the result of mid-19th C restoration – the actual layout also dating from that time. There are extensive yew hedges and some fine specimen trees, including three rough-barked Arizona Cypresses, the tallest of this tender cypress in England.

Best time of year
Worth a visit at any season.

Other highlights
Clipped Irish Yew, **Cedar of Lebanon** and **lime** line the West Drive; some decapitated **Coast Redwoods** fringe the South Drive. There are also a **Monterey Cypress** of record size, plus two young ones. By the 19th-C stable block are some large golden yews.

Flanking rows of clipped Irish Yews in the north garden are trees of a hybrid thorn, *Crataegus × lavallei,* which make round heads in contrast to the erect yews.

Continued on page 102.
Continued on page 102.

THE SOUTH EAST

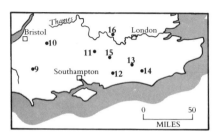

WILTSHIRE

9 Lacock Abbey

LOCATION **Just east of A350, 3 miles (5 km) south of Chippenham;** *Landranger Sheet 173, ST919684;* OPEN **(grounds only) Apr to end-Oct: every day 2-6;** ADMISSION **(grounds and cloisters only) £0.60.**

L acock Abbey is generally associated with William Henry Fox Talbot, pioneer of modern photography. This versatile man was also an eminent botanist and in the mid-19th C he was responsible for planting several notable exotics in these grounds. A century earlier, his great-grandfather, John Ivory Talbot, had extensively changed the design of the grounds, building the ha-ha and reclaiming some parkland to make the laid-out garden which is seen today.

Best time of year

In late spring the fine **Judas Tree** on the South Terrace produces beautiful pea-like rose-pink flowers. By autumn these have become attractive purple seed pods.

The **Swamp Cypress** by the ornamental pond produces spectacular autumn colouring, as does a specimen by the museum and a nearby **Tulip Tree.**

Other highlights

There are two fine **Black Walnuts** from eastern North America along the approach to the Abbey and another specimen just north of it. Towards the orchard grows a Nettle Tree, and across the path can be seen an **Indian Bean Tree,** both of which also originate in North America. Some unusually large **plane** trees planted by Fox Talbot complete the scene.

10 Stourhead

LOCATION **At Stourton, on the B3092, 3 miles (5 km) north-west of Mere (A303);** *Landranger Sheet 183, ST7735;* OPEN **(garden only) all year: every day 8-7 or sunset if earlier;** ADMISSION **(garden only) Mar to mid-May, mid-Jun to end-Nov £1.50. Mid-May to mid-Jun £2. Dec to end-Feb £0.80.**

S tourhead, with its pleasure garden, lakes and temples, is one of the finest examples of 18th-C landscape design in the country. The shores of the lake and the lower woodlands contain perhaps the most magnificent tree specimens, including many rarities. Throughout a period of 200 years, consecutive members of the Hoare family have modified the garden, and their work is testament to the influence which exotic trees, particularly conifers, can have on British gardens.

Best time of year

Beautiful throughout the year.

Other highlights

Trees from North America, Japan, Eurasia and China dominate: this is an unsuitable location for tender specimens.

Walking south-west from the house towards the pleasure gardens, look out for **Tulip Tree,** American **Red Oak, Katsura Tree** and yellow-leaved sycamore. Towards the Temple of Apollo on the south shore of Garden Lake, interesting exotics include the tallest **Tiger Tail Spruce** in Britain, as well as one of the tallest **Coast Redwoods.** Also present are **Monterey Cypress,** Western Hemlock, **wellingtonia.** Weeping Ash, European Larch, a pale gold form of **Lawson Cypress,** Golden Poplar and two very old trees: a **Tulip Tree** and a **Cedar of Lebanon,** both planted nearly 200 years ago. **Magnolia** also occurs in this part of the garden.

Notable exotics to the right of the stone bridge include **Caucasian Fir,** a golden form of Western Red Cedar, **Delavay's Silver Fir,** a 20-ft (6-m) 'dwarf' Hinoki Cypress, **Paper-bark Maple** and a prominent Weeping Ash. Farther along this woodland garden are some more magnificent conifers; a very large **Noble Fir,** one of the most impressive **Macedonian Pines** anywhere; a 70-ft (21-m) Forrest's Fir and a group of **Dawn Redwoods. Tree of Heaven** and **Snake-bark Maple** also occur, as does **Smooth Japanese Maple** at the head of the lake.

In the pinetum on the north-west shore, interesting exotics include a 65-ft (20-m) Japanese White Pine, Chinese

Fir, Veitch's Silver Fir and California Nutmeg. Farther south, towards the Pantheon, grow the biggest recorded **Nootka Cypress**; two cultivars of **Lawson Cypress; morinda; Oriental Spruce; Swamp Cypress** and Western Hemlock; and along the shore of Turner's Paddock Lake there are **wellingtonias** and a large-leaved poplar from west China.

HAMPSHIRE

11 The Vyne

LOCATION **Off the A340, between Sherborne St John and Bramley, 4 miles (6.5 km) north of Basingstoke;** *Landranger Sheet 175 or 186, SU637566;* OPEN **Apr to mid-Oct: Tues to Thurs, Sat and Sun 2-6. Bank holiday Mon 11-6;** *Closed* **Tues following bank holiday Mon;** ADMISSION **(garden only) £0.80, children £0.40.**

Substantial planting at The Vyne took place in the 19th C when Wigget Chute destroyed all trace of the formal garden likely to have been there since Tudor times.

The parkland contains some lovely old trees, but has never been formally landscaped. The Vyne's soil is neutral to acid, and the northern area of the garden is subject to strong cold winds, thus affecting the planting there. The high water table and close proximity of the main lake (to the west of the house) ensure adequate soil moisture in the garden, even during dry spells.

Best time of year

It is worth visiting The Vyne for its ornamental trees at any time of year. In spring, look out in particular for Snowy Mespil, ornamental crab and various **cherries** to the east of the house); by June **Indian Bean Tree** and several **Locust Trees** (to the west) are looking especially attractive; later on, the delicious fruit of **Black Mulberry** (in the north-east of the garden) ripens into a deep wine red; and by autumn **Sweet Gum, Persian Ironwood** and *Crataegus × prunifolia* are producing magnificent multi-coloured foliage.

Other highlights

Some lovely old phillyrea grow by the chapel and nearby are several **Black Walnut.** To the north of the house common walnut is found along with **Cedar of Lebanon** and orange-twig willow. Peking Willow 'Tortuosa' flourishes in the Wild Garden; by the lake search for **Golden Weeping Willow** (on the south bank) and **Swamp Cypress** and silver willow (on the north bank).

The only exotic of note in the parkland is a corkscrew oak, which can be seen from the garden.

WEST SUSSEX

12 Petworth

LOCATION **Near the junction of the A272 and the A283, 5½ miles (9 km) east of Midhurst;** *Landranger Sheet 197, SU 976218;* OPEN **(house and pleasure grounds) Apr to end-Oct: Tues to Thurs, Sat and Sun and bank holiday Mon 2-6;** *Closed* **Tues following bank holiday Mon; (park only) all year round: daily 9-sunset;** ADMISSION **(house and pleasure grounds) £2, children £1, Connoisseurs' Day (every Tues) £2.50, children £1.25. Free entry to the park.**

The park at Petworth is a remarkable example of an unspoilt 18th-C landcape and contains many magnificent specimen trees. The undulating parkland, designed and planted in the 1750s by 'Capability' Brown, is one of the finest in Britain. The beautiful pleasure grounds were originally laid out in the 16th C and were extensively altered in the 19th C and later. Ideal growing conditions have enabled several trees to attain record heights.

Best time of year

Petworth contains trees that are at their best in spring, summer and autumn, so a visit will be memorable at any of these seasons.

Other highlights

Spectacularly high exotics – often the tallest of their species in Britain – are: Oriental Beech, 63 ft (19 m), *Catalpa × erubescens,* 80 ft (24 m), **Tiger Tail Spruce,** a **magnolia** *(M. kobus)* that has attained 57 ft (17 m) and a beautifully barked birch from China 60 ft (18 m). They are all to be seen in the pleasure grounds, as are several specimens of **Tulip Tree, Red Oak** and **magnolia.** There are also numerous other exotics of interest within this area, but along the east side of the grounds look out especially for **Sweet Gum, Box Elder,**

Locust Tree and **wellingtonia** from North America; **Maidenhair Tree** from China; **Smooth Japanese Maple** and **Snowbell Tree** from Japan; **Holm Oak** and Cornelian Cherry from Europe.

Towards the edge of the woods grow **Persian Ironwood**, tupelo, **Manna Ash, Red** and **Silver Maple, Cedar of Lebanon** and **Oriental Spruce**. The Ionic Rotunda is surrounded by **Handkerchief Tree** and Oriental Beech, and in and around Tanner's Croft Paddock are found **Cider** and **Sweet Gum,** Common and Japanese Walnut, **Caucasian Wing-nut** and **Atlas Cedar.**

In the centre of the pleasure grounds stands the Doric Temple, where trees of note include **Katsura Tree, Japanese Cherry,** Umbrella Tree, **Silver pendent Lime,** Oriental Plane, **Oriental Spruce** and Grand Fir.

Finally, around the lawn and shrubbery near the house, look out for 'Dawyck' Beech, Hop Hornbeam, **Hungarian Oak,** madrona and **Indian Bean Tree.**

13 Nymans Garden

LOCATION **Either side of B2114 at Handcross, off the M23/A23, 4½ miles (7 km) south of Crawley;** *Landranger Sheet 187, TQ265294;* OPEN **Apr to end-Oct: Tues to Thurs, Sat and Sun and bank holiday Mon 11-7 (or sunset if earlier);** *Closed* **Good Fri;** ADMISSION **£1.30, children £0.65.**

This famous garden has a character and charm based on the continuity of management and the personality of three generations of owners; with its large and complex botanical collection, built up over the past 100 years, it is a plantman's paradise, and the trees named here are but a small selection of the rare trees from all over the world. Many rare species were introduced in the 1920s as a result of the expeditions of Forrest, Rock and Kingdon-Ward, but it was the exploits of Harold Comber, which gave Nymans its richest botanical heritage.

Although hybridisation has occurred, there is a low proportion of cultivars: the emphasis has been on experimenting with wild species. The garden is not as frosty as might be expected for this part of Sussex, and some tender trees are in evidence. A pinetum was established in 1896, and to the east is a valley planted with a scattered arboretum. The south-facing land across the road is known as The Rough.

Best time of year
Gloriously colourful during spring, summer and autumn.

Other highlights
The **magnolia** collection is of national importance. There are 45 taxa, including Nyman's most famous **magnolia** hybrid *M. Kobus loebneri* 'Leonard Messel'. Eucryphia is also a speciality and *E.* × *nymansensis* was created here. There are 29 taxa of *Acer.* **Smooth Japanese Maple** makes the biggest impact on the garden, but botanically the most important species is pseudo **Snake-bark Maple,** *A. stachyophyllum.* Other interesting tree collections include False Beech *(Nothofagus),* Horse

Chestnut, **juniper** and **pine** (many specimens being the tallest of their species in the country). The foliage variants of **Hinoki Cypress** are some of the best to be seen anywhere. Some other notable conifers or their cultivars are a 60-ft (16-m) Italian Cypress; an immense Japanese Red Cedar; **Serbian** and **Oriental Spruce** and **Eastern Hemlock.** False Cypress is strongly represented in the pinetum, and in The Rough occur three large **Macedonian Pine,** a 45-ft (14-m) **Lawson Cypress** 'Pottenii' and Chilean **Incense Cedar.**

Throughout the garden, look out for rare or interesting broad-leaved exotics such as 'Dawyck' Beech, Pride of India, Philodendron, photinia, Pagoda Tree, **Snowbell Tree, Monkey Puzzle,** variegated **Indian Bean Tree,** bitternut, **Cork Oak,** yellow catalpa and many **rowans** including **Hupeh.**

EAST SUSSEX

14 Sheffield Park Garden

LOCATION **East of the A275, midway between Lewes and East Grinstead;** *Landranger Sheet 198, TQ415240;* OPEN **Apr to 9 Nov: Tues to Sat 11-6; Sun and bank holiday Mon 2-6;** *Closed* **Tues following bank holidays, all other Mons and Good Friday;** ADMISSION **May, Oct and Nov £2.50, children £1.30. Apr, June to end-Sept £1.90, children £1.**

Sheffield Park's arboretum boasts many rare specimens, great variety and magnificent autumn colour: it is worth a whole day's outing. Set around five lakes, conditions are wet, and fertile soil supports both deciduous and coniferous trees. The original landscape was designed by 'Capability' Brown, who sculpted the two Women's Way ponds. Humphry Repton was responsible in 1789 for a string of lakes that were later enlarged to become the Ten Foot Pond and Middle Lake. The more delicate varieties of tree favour the south-facing area of the garden to the north of these two lakes.

The illustration on the cover of this book is from Sheffield Park.

Best time of year

To see this garden at its best, visit in autumn when it is magnificently coloured by many exotics, especially by tupelo, or Black Gum, and by Japanese Maple. Other colourful exotic trees include **Sweet Gum**, North American **Scarlet Oak**, False Beech *(Nothofagus antarctica)*, **medlar** and **Swamp Cypress**. In many cases there are literally hundreds of these species, very few of which have reached full maturity.

Other highlights

More than a hundred varieties of conifer include the Monterey Pine, **Brewer's Weeping Spruce** from Oregon, and **wellingtonia**. Also: two **Cider Gums** from Tasmania, reaching about 100 ft (30 m) in height; Red Cedar and golden larch from Japan; **Serbian Spruce; Chinese Juniper; Oriental Spruce; Cedar of Lebanon; Eastern Hemlock, Smooth Arizona Cypress** and **Coast Redwood** from North America. Also glorious during spring are the **magnolias** *(M. kobus* and *M. tripetala)*.

SURREY

15 Winkworth Arboretum

LOCATION **On the east side of the B2130, 3 miles (5 km) south-east of Godalming;** *Landranger Sheet 186, SU990412;* OPEN **every day during daylight hours;** ADMISSION **May and Oct to mid-Nov £1. At other times £0.80. Children £0.30 all year round.**

This landscaped arboretum is notable among National Trust properties for being designed and created by just one person, Dr Wilfrid Fox, who purchased the grounds in 1937. The collection is presented in a novel way: for most of the trees are not planted singly, but in groups, which adds greatly to the dramatic effect.

Winkworth is set on a steep hillside, with two artificial lakes below. The climate is fairly severe compared with other gardens in southern England; consequently hardy plants from China, Japan, Europe, Eurasia and eastern North America predominate.

Best time of year

Dr Fox planted Winkworth mainly for its autumn colour, for which it is now justly famous. He based his scheme on **maple:** look for **Red Maple**, Nikko, **Snake-bark** Norway and especially Downy and **Smooth Japanese Maple.** Other exotics displaying beautiful multi-coloured foliage are Snowy Mespil, Yellow Birch, Shagbark Hickory, **Sweet Gum**, tupelo or Black Gum, **Red, Scarlet** and **Pin Oak**, all from

North America; Japanese Walnut, **cherry**, Large-leaved and Erman's Birch and **Katsura Tree**, from Japan; Antarctic Beech from Chile; **Persian Ironwood;** Transcaucasian Birch; Copper and 'Dawyck' Beech; ornamental apple and ornamental cherry. *Sorbus* is another major speciality. The arboretum holds the national collection of *Sorbus* sections of *aria* and *micromeles* and in autumn the many species display not only excellent foliage but yellow, white, pink, purple and red berries. Those to search for include **Hupeh Rowan,** Common and Swedish Whitebeam, Wild, True and Bastard Service Tree and many cultivars of rowan.

Other highlights

As a foil to all these colours, blue **Atlas Cedar** has been extensively planted. Other widespread ornamental trees are numerous cultivars of **cherry,** holly and **magnolia.** These occur mainly in the Bowl and the Slopes, Holly Wood and Magnolia Wood respectively. These areas, and the Summer Garden, provide flowering trees in both spring and summer. In these areas also look out for *Eucryphia* × *nymansensis,* **Indian Bean Tree, Snowbell Tree, Foxglove Tree** and **Hungarian Oak.**

In the Foliage Glade occur variegated Sweet Chestnut, poplar from China, Silver Weeping Pear and variegated **Tulip Tree.** Nearby in the Alpine Meadow are two magnificent False, or Southern, Beeches from Chile – the deciduous raoul and the evergreen *Nothofagus dombeyi.*

Amongst many other trees of note not already mentioned are Sorrel Tree (on Sorbus Hill), several rare ashes and beeches (on Winkworth Hill), magnificent **Silver Lime** and **Lawson Cypress** (in Memorial Glade) and **Strawberry Tree,** madrona and **Handkerchief Tree** (on the Azalea steps).

BERKSHIRE

16 Cliveden

LOCATION **Two miles (3 km) north of Taplow, on the B476, off the A40;** *Landranger Sheet 175, SU913856;* OPEN **(grounds only) Mar to end-Dec: every day 11-6 or sunset if earlier;** ADMISSION **£2.00, children £1, except Mon, Tues and Wed (not bank holiday Mon), when it is £1.50, children £0.75.**

Cliveden is one of the National Trust's largest gardens and the most historically varied, providing not only horticultural but also architectural interest. It is a landscaped garden, first planted in the 18th C, and still being added to in order to ensure continued interest. The rides and avenues consist largely of lime, but within this framework there are many specimen trees of breath-taking beauty. The woods contain mainly beech and yew.

The house (once the home of the Astor family) is now an hotel, but part of the building is open to the public on Thursday and Sunday p.m., April to October.

Best time of year

In spring **magnolias** are in bloom; in summer, the Ilex Grove is transformed; and the autumn colours – especially in the Hanging Wood above Cliveden Reach – are unforgettable.

Other highlights

A plant of unusual holly, *Ilex fargesii,* grows on the bank to the west of the house. It has narrow oblong leaves and is one of the largest of its kind in England. Further down the escarpment, a fine specimen of butter nut is similarly distinguished. On the riverside stand several **Swamp Cypresses** and a vigorous young **Tulip Tree** not far from an old specimen reaching 100 ft (30 m). Between these, a sycamore has reached the proportions of a noble tree.

Exotics near the house include two **Black Mulberries,** two Cypress Oaks, **Locust Tree** and **magnolia** *(M. campbellii* and *M. grandiflora).* In the water garden are Pfitzer Juniper, **Sweet Gum** from Mexico; Chinese Thuja and Pagoda, or Scholar's, Tree from China, plus more **magnolias** and many **maples.** Nearby are cultivars of **Indian Bean Tree** and both **Eastern** and Western **Hemlock,** all from North America.

In the Ilex Grove, amongst **Holm Oak,** stands a fine specimen of Common Yew, and nearby thrives an Oriental Plane – a cutting from the famous tree at Blickling Hall, Norfolk. Also to be seen are **Handkerchief Tree;** and a semi-circle of Norway Spruce formed of layered branches from an old tree which recently fell.

In the woods are two **Coast Redwoods; wellingtonia; Turkey Oak; cedars,** including **Japanese Red Cedar; Lawson Cypress, Nootka Cypress** and Grand Fir.

WALES

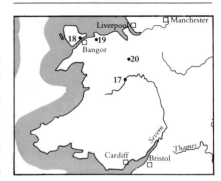

POWYS

17 Powis Castle

LOCATION **One mile (1.5 km) south of Welshpool on the A483;** *Landranger Sheet 126, SJ216064;* OPEN **(garden only) May to end-June: Wed to Sun 1-5.30. July to end-Aug: every day 12-6. Sept: Wed to Sun 1-6. All bank holiday Mon: 11.30-6;** ADMISSION **(garden only) £1.30, children £0.50.**

Powis Castle is situated dramatically on a south-east-facing hillside overlooking the valley of the River Severn. Castle and terraces are built on limestone, while the rest of the garden and the woodland are on a parallel ridge of lime-free soil. The grounds are known for their yew topiary and for their dramatic series of early-18th-C 'hanging gardens' or terraces, each running for about 150 yd (140 m) directly below the Castle. The property is characterized by the contrast between this formality and the surrounding informality.

Best time of year
Good all year round.

Other highlights
Oaks grow to enormous proportions at Powis, **Turkey Oak** occuring as large trees in the Wilderness as does **Lucombe Oak** and **Cork Oak.** Laburnum is another speciality, Scotch Laburnum among those represented. Other broad-leaved exotics include 18 taxa of *Acer* two forms of **Handker-chief Tree,** True Service Tree, holly from Japan and a fine **Strawberry Tree.**

    Maidenhair Tree from China grows on the entrance slopes and at the base of the slopes. Nearby are several **hiba** and a twin-stemmed pendulous form of **Nootka Cypress.** Other notable exotic conifers are **Hinoki Cypress** and **Sawara Cypress,** both from Japan, and **Lawson Cypress, Coast Redwood** and **Eastern Hemlock** from North America. **Deodars** also grow well. By the pool is a group of three very tall **Caucasian Firs,** the biggest being 135 ft (41 m), which makes it one of the finest in the British Isles.

GWYNEDD

18 Plas Newydd

LOCATION **One mile (1.5 km) south-west of Llanfairpwll, Anglesey, on the A4080;** *Landranger Sheets 114 and 115, SH521696;* OPEN **Apr to end-Sept: Sun to Fri 12-5. Oct: Sun to Fri 2-5;** ADMISSION (garden only) **£0.80, children £0.45.**

Damp atmosphere, fertile soil and the frost-preventing waters of the Gulf Stream provide, at Plas Newydd, an ideal habitat for tender and exotic flowering trees, and these have been planted extensively since the 1920s. There is also an arboretum. The present garden layout was conceived in the late-18th C and early-19th C when massive tree-planting and landscaping occurred, partly under the influence of Humphry Repton.

Best time of year
Spring, for the truly memorable collection of flowering trees at their best in full bloom. These include **Tulip Tree, Snowbell Tree,** flowering **cherry, magnolia** and quince.

Other highlights
The exotic delights of Plas Newydd are displayed at their best in the 'West Indies' – the gardens immediately to the south of the house. With a sharp eye, you will find **Atlas Cedar, Monterey Cypress, Cedar of Lebanon, Katsura Tree, Red Oak, Maidenhair Tree** and numerous Japanese Maples. Sloping towards the south-east, these woods surround a beautiful glade filled with many of the flowering trees. Further to the south are yet more flowering trees together with phillyrea, Japanese Maple and an ancient oak, surrounded by a seat, which makes a useful resting place. At the end of the 'West Indies' is the Long Walk containing an unusual and beautiful avenue of **Sawara Cypress** from Japan.

    Magnolia can also be found in the rhododendron garden to the north-east of the house, along the Menai Strait.

19 Bodnant Garden

LOCATION **Half-a-mile (0.8 km) along the Eglwysbach road off the A470, 8 miles (13 km) south of Llandudno;** *Landranger Sheets 115 and 116, SH801723;* OPEN **mid-Mar to end-Oct: every day 10-5;** ADMISSION **£1.50, children £0.80.**

Bodnant's setting, design and plants have given it international acclaim. The planting reflects the tastes and personalities of four generations of owners and three of head gardeners, who have made famous the continuing partnership of Aberconway and Puddle. The garden slopes to the west and is dissected by a deep valley (called 'the Dell') of a tributary of the River Conwy. There is series of ponds in the south. The proximity to mountains results in high rainfall and lower sunshine levels than on the nearby coast. Growth is therefore lush, and liable to winter damage. The garden has magnificent collections of **magnolia,** eucryphia and conifer, as well as an arboretum. The conifers in the Dell form a unique feature: practically nowhere else in Britain can one view such a range of tall specimens from above.

Best time of year
The vast range of **magnolia** (63 taxa), combined with encryphia, flowering **cherry** and ornamental **crab** make a splendid sign in spring. Most spectacular of all is the laburnum tunnel, which dates from the 1880s. Autumn is also impressive, with every tree aflame in yellow, red, russet or coral from *Acer* (49 taxa), **Sweet Gum** from Mexico,

oriental **Sweet Gum** and False Beech – and many others.

Other highlights

Conifers are the oldest exotics planted at Bodnant and are the most impressive of all the trees. Their emphasis, because they were planted prior to the Chinese introductions, is on North American (especially west-coast), European and Japanese taxa. There are over 80 varieties of conifer including Low's Fir, Grand Fir, **Beautiful Fir** and **Noble Fir; Brewer's Weeping Spruce; Western Yellow Pine** and Weymouth Pine; Western, **Eastern** and **Mountain Hemlock; wellingtonia** and **Coast Redwood,** all from North America. There are also **Sawara** and **Hinoki Cypress** from Japan, Chinese Fir, **Maidenhair Tree** and **Dawn Redwood** from China, Mexican White Pine, Plum-fruited Yew from Chile and **Grecian Fir.**

By contrast, broad-leaved exotics include many trees from Japan and China, for example **Snowbell Tree** and **Handkerchief Tree** as well as many of the *Acer.* Most of the 43 taxa of **rowan** are concentrated in the arboretum, which is bisected by two drives.

CLWYD

20 Chirk Castle

LOCATION Half-a-mile (0.8 km) west of Chirk village, off the A5; *Landranger Sheet 117, SJ269381;* OPEN May to end-Sept: Sun, Tues, Wed and Thurs 12-5. Also all Sun in April and all bank holiday Mon 12-5. Oct: Sat and Sun 12-5; ADMISSION £1.60, children £0.55.

The chief glory of Chirk is the flowering trees, most of which have been introduced in recent years. William Emes, a disciple of 'Capability' Brown, designed this open landscape, informally planted, in the 1760s. The clipped yews and hedges, which have become such a prominent feature, were planted in the late-19th C. Though the climate is mild, the Castle stands in an exposed position on rather poor, acidic soil.

Best time of year

Spring and early summer, when the trees in the shrub garden are most spectacular. These include **magnolia, Sargent's Cherry,** Willow-leaved Pear, **Handkerchief Tree** and a rare flowering **ash.**

Other highlights

In the upper lawn area are some magnificent exotics such as **Silver Pendent Lime,** a willow-leaved **magnolia,** Norway Maple, **Tulip Tree** and the early flowering Cornelian Cherry. There are also outstanding large flowering specimens of *Eucryphia* × *nymanensis* and *cornus nuttallii.* The largest tree is a **Cedar of Lebanon,** and towards the ha-ha are two marvellous specimens of Chilean firebush. The niched yew hedge along the terrace probably dates from the 1870s.

The **lime** avenue was designed in the late-17th C to provide an unbroken vista from the Castle to the north. The trees were formerly pollarded to preserve a clear line of foliage.

MIDDLE ENGLAND

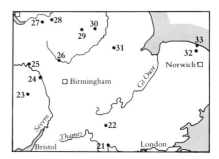

OXFORDSHIRE

21 Greys Court

LOCATION Three miles (5 km) north-west of Henley-on-Thames, on the road to Peppard; *Landranger Sheet 175, SN725834;* OPEN (garden only) Apr to end-Sept: Mon to Sat 2-6. *Closed* **Good Friday; ADMISSION (garden only) £1.30, children £0.65.**

Both house and garden at Greys Court reflect the aspirations of successive families and generations inhabiting the property for nearly a thousand years. The garden is genuinely enchanting and there is a fine undulating park with some marvellous trees.

Best time of year

Spring, when the cherries and the **Foxglove Tree** are in full bloom.

Other highlights

One of the most splendid sights is to the east of the Bachelors Hall, where there are two superb old exotics: a **Tulip Tree** and a Weeping Ash. Both these specimens were planted before 1823, when they appeared in a contemporary print. Nearby is the Old Tithe Barn, the walls of which surround a garden of beautiful **Japanese Cherries;** in the rose garden is a **Foxglove Tree** from China. Leading towards the kitchen garden is an avenue of standard Morello Cherries.

On the east part of the top lawn are several **Strawberry Trees** and further down are an immense Copper Beech by the Chinese bridge, an **Indian Bean Tree, Locust Tree** and a large old Specimen Larch.

Look out for a large **Monkey Puzzle** in the park and a huge **Cedar of Lebanon** in the car park.

BUCKINGHAMSHIRE

22 Waddesdon Manor

LOCATION In Waddesdon village, on the A41, 6 miles (9.5 km) north-west of Aylesbury; *Landranger Sheet 165, SP740169;* OPEN (grounds only) mid-Mar to end-Apr, Oct: Wed to Sat 1-5, Sun 11.30-6. May to Sept: Wed to Sat 1-6, Sun 11.30-6. Good Fri and bank holiday Mon: 11-6; *Closed* Wed following a bank holiday; ADMISSION (grounds and aviary only) £1.00, children £0.25.

The main outlines of the grounds at Waddesdon were laid out by the French landscape gardener, Elie Lainé, in the late-19th C. Thereafter Rothschild and his land bailiff arranged the extensive planting. Many conifers, in-cluding some of the fashionable, recently introduced exotics, were selected, as well as broad-leaves of 30-40 ft (9-12 m) to promote an immediate 'mature' look. This is why some of the trees at Waddesdon are much older than might be expected in grounds laid out only a century ago.

Best time of year
Spring, especially when the Horse Chestnuts are in full bloom.

Other highlights
Most of the interesting exotics are west of the house in Daffodil Valley, where **deodar, Spanish Fir,** blue and ordinary **Atlas Cedar, Oriental Spruce, wellingtonia, Arolla Pine** and a golden form of **Lawson Cypress** all flourish. On the right of the Upper Deer Pen occur Red Horse Chestnut, weep-ing **Japanese Cherry** and **Nootka Cypress;** while **Tulip Tree, Paper-bark Maple** and **Judas Tree** grow well by the Tay Bridge.

Farther north, near the sculpture of Hercules, are Japanese flowering **Crab Apple** and Weeping Cherry, **welling-tonia** and a form of English Yew with horizontal branches. Towards the North Fountain look out for **Macedonian Pine** and Norway Maple and, a little farther on, another impressive blue **Atlas Cedar, Silver Lime** and a weeping form of Copper Beech. Also worth noting are the **Maidenhair Tree, Strawberry Tree** and a variegated form of English Elm near the north-east side of the house.

The open parkland, with its fine views south towards the Chilterns, boasts further interesting exotic specimens including **Cedar of Lebanon,** Crimean Pine, **Noble Fir** and a Chinese thuja (planted by George V). Broad-leaved ornamentals such as **Black Mulberry,** hornbeam, **London Plane** and variegated **Box Elder** are also present.

HEREFORD AND WORCESTER

23 Croft Castle

LOCATION **Five miles (8 km) north-west of Leominster off the A49;** *Landranger Sheet 137, SO455655;* OPEN **Apr and Oct: Sat, Sun and Easter Mon 2-5. May to end-Sept: Wed to Sun and bank holiday Mon 2-6;** ADMISSION **£1.50.**

Croft Castle is 500 years old and its extensive grounds have remained remarkably unchanged over that period; this fact and the fine specimen trees are perhaps the chief reasons for its interest. Even in the 18th C, the planners did not tamper with the basic layout and fine avenues.

Best time of year
Equally attractive at all times of year.

Other highlights
On the wide lawn are many large exotics, including **wellingtonia** and an old **lime tree,** the lower branches of which are rooted in the ground, thus forming a small grove. Between the drive and the short Gothick curtain-wall, impressive **Holm Oaks** grow in the rough turf.

To the west of the house, the open parkland also contains many fine exotic specimens, notably **Coast Redwood, wellingtonia** and **Incense Cedar** from North America and Oriental Plane.

SHROPSHIRE

24 Dudmaston

LOCATION **Half-a-mile (0.8 km) north-west of Quatt, on the west side of the road from Bridgnorth to Kidderminster (A442);** *Landranger Sheet 138, SO746887;* OPEN **Apr to end-Sept: Wed and Sun 2.30-6;** ADMISSION **(garden only) £0.80, children £0.60.**

The Dingle at Dudmaston is a wooded area providing one of the best surviving examples of William Shenstone's style of modest landscaping, as interpreted by Walter Wood in the 18th C. A walk through the Dingle illustrates many phases of the development of the landscape here.

The estate has been in the same family for more than 850 years; among 20th-C owners, Geoffrey Wolryche-Whitmore made a notable contribution to the ornamental planting and he introduced a surprising variety of both broad-leaves and conifers. The park was landscaped in the 18th C and an extensive garden leads down to the main lake.

Best time of year
In spring the garden to the south of the house is at its most attractive, with **magnolia, Japanese Cherry** and Snowdrop Tree in bloom. A group of mature Snowy Mespil by the rockery are also magnificent at this time. Autumn

colour, too, is superb, especially from **Dawn Redwood, Sweet Gum, Paper-bark** and **Red Maple** on the west lawn.

Other highlights
Many of the other exotics of note are also on the west lawn. These include an old willow-leaved pear, **Indian Bean Tree, medlar, Swamp Cypress** and various cultivars of **Lawson Cypress,** which provide a good selection of colour and form. Amongst other interesting trees in the garden look out for mature specimens of **Atlas Cedar, Cedar of Lebanon** and **Black Mulberry** (near the car park).

In the Dingle, some large specimen trees remain from Walter Wood's picturesque landscape planting, notably a huge Cut-Leaf Beech and **Noble Fir.**

25 Attingham Park

LOCATION **On the north side of the road to Telford (A5), 4 miles (6.5 km) south-east of Shrewsbury;** *Landranger Sheet 126, SJ542093;* OPEN **(deer park and grounds only) all year round: daily during daylight hours;** *Closed* **25 Dec;** ADMISSION **(deer park and grounds only) £0.50, children £0.25.**

The landscaping at Attingham Park began in 1770, when Noel Hill (later first Lord Berwick) commissioned Thomas Leggett to improve the grounds. Leggett created a parkland setting in the style of 'Capability' Brown, with clumps of trees in the open landscape and solid banks of woodland around the boundaries. Noel Hill later built a vast neo-classical mansion surrounding the original building, and it was for this new house that his son, the second Lord Berwick, employed Humphry Repton to devise a further landscaping scheme in 1797. His proposals, contained in a 'Red Book' still at Attingham, were carried out over the following 20 years, and since then few alterations have been made to the landscape.

Both Leggett and Repton preferred to use traditional woodland species in the parkland, so it is in the Pleasure Grounds immediately surrounding the house that the ornamental trees are found. These are confined to two areas: the Spring Garden, and the Mile Walk along the bank of the River Tern, which makes a marvellous stroll.

Best time of year
Spring. Also autumn, when honeylocust, **red oak** and thorn all from North America, contribute – among others – to the wide range of foliage colours.

Other highlights
Two of the main attractions at Attingham are an avenue of False Acacia, near the Walled Garden, and a magnificent grove of immense **Cedar of Lebanon,** which protects the north-east of the house. Beyond the cedars is the Mile Walk, where you should find **Tulip Tree** from North America, Himalayan tree cotoneaster and a formal circle of *Gleditsia triacanthos* planted as a memorial in 1967.

Exotics of interest in the Spring Garden include Snowy Mespil.

STAFFORDSHIRE

26 Shugborough

LOCATION Five-and-a-half miles (9 km) south-east of Stafford on the A513; *Landranger Sheet 127, SJ992225;* OPEN mid-Mar to end-Oct: Tues to Fri and bank holiday Mon 10.30-5.30. Sat and Sun 2-5.30; ADMISSION (grounds only) £1 per vehicle (NT members included).

Shugborough has an **oak** arboretum, established in 1975, in which nearly all the uncommon oak species are grouped, region by region, on an island. Other interesting exotics of varying ages are scattered around the garden and park. The garden was laid out when the present house was built, at the end of the 17th C, and the island in the River Sow was formed about a century later. There was extensive tree-planting in the 19thC, especially after the 2nd Earl of Lichfield had inherited the estate.

The house, dating from 1693, has some fine French furniture and relics of Admiral Anson, the navigator.

Best time of year
Maple and **oak** are specialities, and their foliage looks magnificent in autumn. Most of the exotics can be seen within the garden and island, so look out for **Silver Maple, Smooth Japanese Maple, Cappadocian Maple, Paperbark Maple,** Korean Maple, **Red Maple** and **Box Elder** as well as **oak** from North America, Europe and Asia. American **Red Oak** and **Scarlet Oak** can also be found in the park.

Other highlights
Variegated yew and topiary of golden yew grow to the west of the house and **Golden Weeping Willow** along the river. Another fine specimen of golden yew occurs towards the Doric Temple, where there is also Copper Beech and Variegated Holly. Along the river path between the Chinese House and Trent Lodge search for Irish Yew and White-bark Himalayan Birch. A Horse Chestnut with boughs that have layered themselves grows by the museum, and its cultivar 'Baummannii' is nearby. On the Ladies Walk are found Paper-bark and White-bark Himalayan Birch, Weeping Holly and sycamore cultivars. Other broad-leaves of interest include **Tulip Tree, Silver Lime,** Caucasian Lime, purple-stemmed High-clere Holly 'Hodginsii', laburnum, several sizeable **Common Limes** and cultivars of flowering **cherry.** Exotic conifers include **Swamp Cypress, deodar** and mature **Cedar of Lebanon.**

There is plenty of note in the park surrounding the walled garden, particularly **wellingtonia, Noble Fir, Oriental Spruce,** juniper, Chinese Cat's Tail Pine, **Handkerchief Tree** and several marvellous Horse Chestnut. Walking back north towards the house you can also see Norway Maple 'Schwedleri', Sugar Maple and **Pin Oak;** Cut-leaf Beech and an immense red-twigged lime.

Other notable exotics scattered around the park are **Silver Pendent Lime, Holm Oak, Turkey Oak,** many sizeable hawthorns, red Horse Chestnut, the rare Sunrise Horse Chestnut, Italian alder, False, or Southern, Beech and many pines.

CHESHIRE

27 Tatton Park

LOCATION On the A5034, 1½ miles (2.5 km) north-east of its junction with the A50, and 3 miles (5 km) north of Knutsford; *Landranger Sheet 109, SJ737815;* OPEN (garden only) Apr to mid-May and Sept to end-Oct: Mon to Sat 11.30-5. Sun and bank holiday Mon 10.30-5.30. Mid-May to end-Aug: Mon to Sat 11-5.30. Sun and bank holiday Mon 10.30-6. Nov to end-Mar: Mon to Sat 1-4. Sun and bank holiday Mon 12-4; *Closed* 25 Dec; ADMISSION (garden only) summer £0.80, winter £0.60.

Almost half the tree taxa in this garden are conifers and there is an important pinetum and arboretum. The number of cultivars and hybrids is also impressive and this reflects the property's ornamental interest; Japanese plants predominate. The garden is set within an extensive landscaped park, planned partly by Humphry Repton. Sir John Paxton designed the terraced Italian Garden. Within the garden are also an orangery, a fernery and an authentic Japanese garden, probably the best example of its type in Britain.

The house itself is an exceptionally fine 18th-C mansion.

Best time of year
Spring, also autumn, with the multi-coloured foliage from countless trees, but especially **maple,** which is a speciality.

Other highlights

Broad-leaved exotics planted generally around the garden include several young Erman's Birch, Japanese Large-leaved Birch, **Common Lime,** Double Gean Cherry, **Snowbell Tree** and **magnolia.** Of the conifers, **Lawson Cypress** and its cultivars are extensively planted, but are less important than **Sawara Cypress,** which is another of Tatton's specialities. Also look out for **hiba, Coast Redwood, wellingtonia,** Western Hemlock and two rarely seen **hemlocks,** *Tsuga sieboldii* and *T. chinensis.*

Specimen conifers of interest on the lawns below the house are **deodar, Brewer's Weeping Spruce,** an old **Cedar of Lebanon** and a prominent Korean Fir. **Snake-bark** and red snake-bark **Maple,** Swedish Whitebeam, **Pin Oak, Caucasian Wing-nut,** Wild Service Tree, **Crab Apple, Sargent's Cherry,** Cheal's Weeping Cherry, Chinese Persimmon and topiary of variegated holly also occur here or below in Turner's Mere.

One of the most attractive features of Tatton is the glade of **Dawn Redwood** beside Broad Walk. Prickly castor oil tree, Kentucky coffee tree, *Sorbus glabrescens* and a large American **Red Oak** can also be found.

In the south-east corner of the garden lies the pinetum, where amongst other trees occur **Caucasian** and a good sized Nikko **Fir,** cultivars of **Sawara** and **Nootka Cypress,** Hondo, blue and **Oriental Spruce, morinda** and also **Mountain Hemlock,** plus **Arolla,** Mountain, Weymouth and **Bhutan Pine** – the last two being especially imposing specimens.

Nearby is the Japanese garden. Of note here are hornbeam maple, **Smooth Japanese Maple** and cultivars, Yoshino cherry, weeping juniper and **Japanese Red Cedar.** Between here and the arboretum grow prominent **Swamp Cypresses,** pendent rowan and a 20-ft (6-m) fastigiate **Atlas Cedar.** The arboretum contains several cultivars of **Crab Apple,** a large Père David's maple and a rare fastigiate silver birch.

28 Dunham Massey

LOCATION **Off the A56, 3 miles (5 km) south-west of Altrincham;** *Landranger Sheet 109, SJ735874;* OPEN **(garden only) Apr to end-Oct: Mon to Thurs 12-5.30. Sat, Sun and bank holiday Mon 11-5.30;** ADMISSION £2.00.

Much work has recently been done in the formal garden on the north front at Dunham Massey in order to restore it to its former glory of 1906, created by the 9th Countess of Stamford. Elsewhere the Victorian layout dominates alongside traces of 17th and 18th-C ones.

Dunham Massey has a vibrant garden with an excellent mix of mature specimens and young trees planted in the last few years, and many more exotics being introduced as time goes on; generous plantings of **rowan** and birch, for example, are planned.

Best time of year

Some notable ornamental trees at flower in early summer, and the autumn foliage can be impressive.

Other highlights

From the very large lawn in the centre of the garden all the following mature trees can be spotted: **Locust Tree, Cork** and **Holm Oak, Cedar of Lebanon** and blue **Atlas Cedar,** all from the Mediterranean; **Tulip Tree, Red Oak** and **Swamp Cypress** from North America. You should also be able to identify sycamore 'Brilliantissimum', mulberry and **Lucombe Oak** as well as an impressive variegated oak.

Less prominent, but equally interesting are the recently-planted specimens of Japanese Dogwood, Père David's Maple, **Katsura** and **Maidenhair Trees** from the Far East; **Sweet Gum** and **Silver Maple** 'Laciniatum' from North America; Cut-leaf Beech and *Tilia tuan.* All these trees are scattered throughout the garden.

In the park are fine specimens of variegated beech and **Common Lime.**

DERBYSHIRE

29 Hardwick Hall

LOCATION **Nine-and-a-half miles (15 km) south-east of Chesterfield – approach from M1 Junction 29 on the A617;** *Landranger Sheet 120, SK463638;* OPEN **(garden only) Apr to end-Oct: every day 12-5.30;** ADMISSION **(garden only) £1.20, children £0.60.**

Hardwick Hall is situated on a prominent escarpment and the resulting exposure to high winds can cause severe problems. There is a formal garden with three walled courtyards containing some fine exotic specimens.

The house itself is famous as the home of the formidable 'Bess of Hardwick', Countess of Shrewsbury, and for the large number and size of the windows – an innovative feature for what is essentially an Elizabethan mansion. Of particular interest inside are the fine tapestries and needlework; house and grounds together make a full day out.

Best time of year
Lovely at almost any time of year, but bear in mind that spring growth can be retarded on such an exposed site.

Other highlights
Two large **Cedars of Lebanon** dominate the main entrance, in the West Court. They were planted in 1810, whereas in the East Court are two recently-planted specimens; from here, too, a **lime** avenue can be seen receding into the distant parkland.

The main garden area is within the South Court, which is divided into sections. There are some large yews of conical shape; some recent plantings of **Hungarian Oak, Indian Bean Tree** and **Tulip Tree;** and, in the north-west section, **magnolia.** Beside the herb garden in the south-west section is a nuttery, with nut-bearing trees including a mature walnut. On the southern boundary is a mulberry walk; a beautiful **Turkey Oak** spreads its branches along the east wall. The ornamental orchard, in the north-east section, contains pears, apples and **Crab Apples** with the central walk lined by *Malus hupehensis,* the clusters of small yellow and red fruit giving colour in autumn.

NOTTINGHAMSHIRE

30 Clumber Park

LOCATION Four-and-a-half miles (7 km) south-east of Worksop, one mile (1.5 km) from the A1/A57; *Landranger Sheet 120, SU645774;* **OPEN all year dawn until dusk; ADMISSION pedestrians free; cars £1.40. Large-scale maps of the park are available from the Cycle Hire Centre.**

Extending nearly to 4,000 acres, Clumber is one of Britain's most-visited Country Parks. The Park itself was created in the late-18th C by the Dukes of Newcastle out of heathland on the edge of Sherwood Forest. Both Richard Payne Knight and William Sawrey Gilpin played important roles in its design. The variety of scenery within the grounds and the sheer size means that a whole day can happily be spent exploring the many miles of gently undulating roads and tracks – with the attractive option of using bicycles, which are for hire. Near the chapel and lake are quiet Victorian pleasure grounds with sweeping lawns under large specimen trees.

Best time of year
Autumn, with the multi-coloured foliage of the beeches and **oaks,** especially American **Red Oak** on Lincoln Terrace.

Other highlights
From the car park, wander towards the pleasure grounds, which stretch along the lake. There you will see **Swamp Cypress** and **Eastern Hemlock** from the east coast of North America and **Mountain Hemlock** and **wellingtonia** from the west coast. Also present are **Cedars of Lebanon,** acacias from Australia and, at the far end of Lincoln Terrace, **Dawn Redwood,** or Water Fir, from China. From near the chapel an avenue of **Atlas cedars** leads to the massive walled kitchen garden, worth a visit in its own right.

While viewing the parkland, look out for the following exotics south of the classical bridge: **Macedonian Pine, Bhutan Pine, Monkey Puzzle** and an avenue of Copper Beech. Between Carburton Lodge and the car park are **deodar** from the Himalayas and blue **Atlas Cedar** from Africa.

Other exotics of interest are rather scattered among the native trees but they include Weeping Beech (in Blackhill clump), Jeffrey's Pine (in Ash Tree Hill Wood) and **Hungarian Oak** (in Cabin Hill Covert).

LINCOLNSHIRE

31 Belton

LOCATION Three miles (5 km) north-east of Grantham, just off the road to Lincoln – the A607; *Landranger Sheet 121, SK3993;* **OPEN (park and garden only) Apr to end-Oct: Wed to Sun and bank holiday Mon 1-5.30;** *Closed* **all other Mon, Good Fri and all Tues; ADMISSION £2.20, children £1.10; free access to park on foot only from Lion Lodge Gates, from Easter.**

Belton park and gardens were originally laid out around 1700, but various changes have been made over the years by William Eames amongst others. Planting in the park and pleasure ground has been a continuous process and so the trees are of varying age; while most trees around the formal garden arrived in the mid- to late-19th C.

Best time of year
Autumn foliage colour at Belton is magnificent: yellows and red of **maple** and **oak** and russets of beech and **medlar.**

Other highlights
Looking north into the formal garden from the house, notice several fine **Cedars of Lebanon** and various forms of **Atlas Cedar.** Other notable exotics in this area are Purple Sycamore, **Locust Tree, Cappadocian Maple, Tulip Tree,** 'Dawyck' Beech, Golden Irish Yew and **Indian Bean Tree.** Farther to the east are **Swamp Cypress, wellingtonia** and **Coast Redwood.** Near the orangery, to the west of the formal garden, are **medlar** and **magnolia,** and along the drive is a line of Vossii Laburnums.

The Wilderness, which is to the west of the house, contains some immense Weeping Beeches, one of which overhangs the miniature railway, a magnificent sight. With a searching eye, you should also pick out Copper Beech, **Silver Maple** and **London Plane,** both here and elsewhere in the park. **Deodar, Coast Redwood, maple, Red Oak** and Golden Yew are also present.

Prominent exotics in the meadow area to the west and north-west of the car park include **Lucombe Oak.**

NORFOLK

32 Blickling Hall

LOCATION On the north side of the B1354, 1½ miles (2.5 km) northwest of Aylsham; *Landranger Sheet 133, TG188275;* **OPEN Apr to mid-Oct: Tues, Wed, Fri to Sun and bank holiday Mon 12-5;** *Closed* **Good Fri; ADMISSION (garden only) £1.40, children £0.70.**

The colourful herbaceous borders and impressive formal yew hedges (believed to be 350 to 400 years old) are the main attractions at Blickling, but a number of unusual trees also make it well worth a visit. By way of contrast, another side of the house is surrounded by a gentler 18th-C landscape, and there is a lake, which stretches away for a mile to the north.

Best time of year
Either early summer, when the chestnut avenue (in the park) and **magnolia** is in full bloom, or in autumn, when the leaves of many trees, especially **Persian Ironwood** and **Dawn Redwood,** turn gold, crimson, russet or brown.

Other highlights
Not often seen in this part of the country is Fern-leaved Beech, which bears little resemblance to Common Beech. A magnificent **Turkey Oak,** 120 ft (36 m) in height and 240 years old, stands at the south-east end of the lake. There is also an avenue of **Turkey Oak** running across the full width of the formal woodland area of the garden.

Another extremely impressive avenue of trees, Horse Chestnut this time, runs away from the Temple on the far side of the formal garden.

Other prominent trees include a majestic Oriental Plane and **Cedar of Lebanon,** a specimen of the latter situated at the edge of the West Garden being 80 ft (25 m) tall. Also in the West Garden is *Magnolia hypoleuca* and elsewhere in the grounds are more **magnolia** including *M. grandiflora.*

33 Felbrigg Hall

LOCATION Two miles (3 km) southwest of Cromer, off the A148; *Landranger Sheet 133, TG193394;* **OPEN (garden only) Apr to-mid Oct: Sat to Mon, Wed, Thurs 11-5.30; ADMISSION (garden only) £0.40, children £0.20.**

Considering the sea is only two miles (3 km) away, Felbrigg is an oasis of peace and quiet. It is sheltered by the Great Wood planted in the late-17th C by William Windham and its large grounds are filled with unusual exotic trees, for which it is renowned. After wandering around the garden, there are woodland and lakeside walks for the visitor to enjoy.

Best time of year
The beautiful multi-coloured leaves of **Red Oak,** thorn (*Crataegus pinnatifida major* and *C. prunifolia*), **Tulip Tree, Persian Ironwood,** American Rowan and **Sweet Gum** vie for attention with autumn flowers from Chinese Glossy Privet, Autumn Cherry and **Straw-**

berry **Tree.** The walled garden is, however, at its best in spring when mimosa, **medlar,** lilac and many of the ornamental thorns are in bloom.

Other highlights

Around the house are many other broad-leaved exotics, the most notable being **Locust Tree, Turkey** and **Holm Oak,** Weeping and **Manna Ash,** Sweet Bay, Ornamental Pear and some of the most beautiful flowering **cherries** including **Sargent's Cherry** and forms of wild and bird cherry. Of the conifers, **Atlas Cedar, wellingtonia and Lawson Cypress** occur.

A short walk from the house brings you to the walled garden, which contains a collection of ornamental thorns, including some of the most unusual and beautiful species for leaf colour and fruit. Specimens originate from North Africa, North America, Mexico and China. Also of interest are **Black Mulberry,** fig and Pyrenean Oak.

Exotics to search for in the park are Purple Beech, **Black** and Common **Walnut,** sycamore 'Corstorphinense' (on the west side of the estate), **Red Oak** and yet more thorns, especially Midland Hawthorn 'Rosea Flore Pleno'. There was once an avenue of **Common Lime** but only one ancient, deeply furrowed specimen survives. A group of young **limes** have now been established to the south-west of the house.

NORTHERN ENGLAND

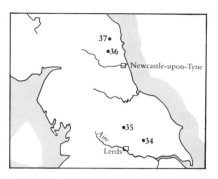

NORTH YORKSHIRE

34 Beningbrough Hall

LOCATION Off the road from York to Shipton (A19), 3 miles (5 km) west of Shipton; *Landranger Sheet 105, SE516586;* **OPEN Apr to end-Oct: Tues to Thurs, Sat and Sun 12-6. Bank holiday Mon 11-6; ADMISSION (gardens and exhibitions only) £1.40, children £0.50.**

The gardens at Beningbrough Hall reflect an amalgamation of different styles of gardening, but the most pronounced is the Victorian including many notable exotics. There is, for example, the 'American Garden' planted in the late-19th C. Earlier, in the late-18th C, W.S. Gilpin produced some designs for the park and garden and, although these were never fully implemented, his influence can still be seen in most areas, beyond the ha-ha.

Best time of year

Spring and early summer in particular,

when **magnolia, Locust Tree,** ornamental **cherry** and **crab** vie for attention.

Other highlights

On the terrace by the house occurs a rare English oak with cream-variegated leaves; nearby are fig and **deodar.** Many trees with interesting barks are planted in the Wilderness, where you should search for **Snake-bark Maple,** a form of Hill Cherry, *Betula jacquemontii,* Cut-leaf Beech and Golden Yew. Visible in the park from this area are **Holm Oak** and **Common Lime.**

Farther east, past the house, are White Mulberry, **medlar** 'Nottingham', Portugal Quince and **Maidenhair Tree;** then comes the Pleasure Ground, where a stately **Turkey Oak, Black Mulberry** and variegated sycamore occur. The American Garden contains many unusual exotics including a rare Cockscomb Beech, purple-leaved **Smooth Japanese Maple,** walnut, **Tulip Tree,** a cultivar of **Silver Maple,** Pencil Cedar, **Eastern Hemlock** and **Western Yellow Pine.**

Other trees of interest in the garden include pollarded Oriental Planes near the restaurant and alternate red- and yellow-flowering Siberian crab beside the Walled Garden; also various exotic **oaks,** especially **Hungarian** and **Cork** (in or near the car park).

35 Studley Royal

LOCATION Off the road to Pateley Bridge – the B6265, 2 miles (3 km) south-west of Ripon; *Landranger Sheet 99, SE271683;* **OPEN Apr to**

end-June and Sept: daily 10-7. July and Aug: daily 10-8. Oct to end-Mar: daily 10-4; *Closed* 24 and 25 Dec; ADMISSION £1.50, children £0.70.

Studley Royal is interesting in that, when the park and water gardens were laid out mainly between 1720 and 1740, only native trees were chosen to ornament the landscape. Many of the original trees planted at this time by John Aislabie still survive. The park contains dispersed plantings of Sweet Chestnut and geometric avenues of a variety of trees, especially **lime,** beech, English and Sessile Oak, while the Water Garden, with its steep sides, is backed by mixed broad-leaf woodland and some striking original Scots Pines on the east side.

Best time of year
Autumn, when the multi-coloured foliage is magnificent.

Other highlights
Among the outstanding specimens in the park are a Field Maple (north-west of the lake); a legendary 500-year-old English Oak and an unusually-old wild cherry (both towards Lindrick Gate); and some immense Sweet Chestnuts, along Seven Bridges valley, east of the lake.

South of the lake is the Water Garden, where you should look out for a particularly fine Scots Pine towering over yew hedges in the north-west corner. Near the Wolfe Monument grows an unusual example of a Shrouded Tree – all lower branches are removed as the tree grows in order to make it tall, straight and with a high, small crown.

Round the corner towards Fountains Abbey occurs a huge sycamore beside the River Skell; and farther along are the Seven Sisters, two surviving specimens of seven large common yews, rumoured to be over 1,200 years old.

NORTHUMBERLAND

36 Wallington

LOCATION **Either side of the B6342, near Cambo, 12 miles (19 km) west of Morpeth;** *Landranger Sheet 81, NZ030843;* OPEN **(grounds) all year round during daylight hours; (walled garden) Apr to end-Sept: every day 10-7. Oct 10-6. Nov to end-Mar 10-4;** ADMISSION **(walled gardens and grounds only) £1, children £0.50.**

Wallington boasts much fine woodland in close proximity to the house. Both East and West Woods were laid out with ponds and planted in 1737-8 by Sir Walter Calverly, who was largely responsible for creating the entire park and gardens. Successive generations of Trevelyans have also been involved in enhancing the beauty of the grounds. Despite its cold climate, Wallington contains some reputedly tender plants.

Best time of year
Wallington is worth a visit at any season.

Other highlights
The walled garden on the east side of the road is full of interest and contains many trees including Norway Maple 'Crimson

King' and Young's Weeping Birch. Small ornamental trees flourishing in this area are **Japanese Cherry,** double-flowered morello cherry, white **magnolia** and many species and varieties of apple, **rowan** and thorn.

In East Wood occur several young trees with tinted foliage – such as yellow-tipped Norway Spruce and coppery-tinted Norway Maple – as well as **Handkerchief Tree, Dawn Redwood** and **Chinese Juniper.** Portico Walk is lined with pairs of **Lawson Cypresses** 'Kilmacurragh'.

On the east lawn can be seen more flowering trees beyond clumps of golden yew; also, **Nootka** and **Lawson Cypress, deodar,** a variegated form of Norway Maple, **Cappadocian Maple** and red-flowered hybrid chestnut. Further round the house are young Copper Beech, **Tulip Tree** and **Cedar of Lebanon.**

37 Cragside

LOCATION **One mile (1.5 km) north of Rothbury, on the B6341, Alnwick road;** *Landranger Sheet 81, NV073022;* OPEN **(country park) Apr to end- Sept: every day 10.30-6. Oct: every day 10.30-5. Nov to end-Mar: Sat and Sun 10.30-4;** ADMISSION **(Country Park only) £1, children £0.50.**

Cragside is set on a steep ragged slope, with informal landscaping right up to the house. Both house and Country Park reflect the genius of the 1st Lord Armstrong who, between 1864 and 1884, is said to have planted some seven million trees to convert rough moorland into the richly wooded pleasure ground that now exists. Many of these trees still survive. There is also a series of artificial lakes above and below the house as well as a medley of intricate paths and well-surfaced drives.

Best time of year
The exotic trees at Cragside are worth a visit at any season.

Other highlights
Conifers predominate in this property and some of those from North America especially are amongst the tallest in the country. The most widespread include **Noble Fir,** Low's Fir and **Lawson Cypress** from North America, also **Caucasian Fir.** Other trees of note scattered around the grounds include Western and **Mountain Hemlock; Nootka Cypress; Colorado White Fir** and **wellingtonia** from North America; Mountain and **Arolla Pine** and **Spanish Fir** from Europe and **Oriental Spruce.** There is a superb Californian Red Fir along the stream and within a comparatively short distance of the house can also be found **Monkey Puzzle** from Chile; **Sawara Cypress** and **Tiger-tail Spruce** from Japan; **Eastern Hemlock,** Blue and Colorado Spruce from North America; Golden Yew, **Grecian Fir** and a golden form of Norway Spruce.

SCOTLAND

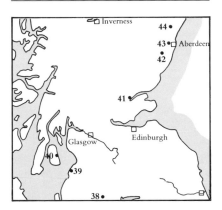

DUMFRIES & GALLOWAY

38 Threave Garden

LOCATION **One mile (1.5 km) west of Castle Douglas, off the road from Dumfries (A75);** *Landranger Sheet 84, NX7362;* OPEN **all year round: daily 9-sunset;** ADMISSION **£1.20, children £0.60.**

Threave is a comparatively young garden with all the ornamentals having been planted since 1960, when the gardening school opened there. The garden is situated in 60 acres of parkland surrounding Threave House and boasts an arboretum as well as several other tree collections scattered around the garden.

Best time of year
Spring, when **crab** and **cherry** make a striking display.

Other highlights
The area from the main gate to the car

park contains some of the largest trees, with mature specimens of **Beautiful Fir** and Western Hemlock from western North America; also **Oriental Spruce.** A fine specimen of fastigiate hornbeam is near the gate, plus a collection of **Lawson Cypress** cultivars. Farther on is the **crab** and **cherry** collection and a small collection of poplar and **gum.** After passing through the Visitor Centre, look out for a marvellous Weeping Ash and, in the Woodland Garden, embothrium, eucryphia and a magnificent **Maidenhair Tree.**

A dwarf conifer collection is near the Sunken Garden and in the arboretum is an interesting collection of alder, including Italian red and grey, also *Alnus maximowiczii.* The *Sorbus* collection and a collection of pines and firs brings you to the Heather Garden alongside which is the main **gum** collection. A fascinating group of holly – some 25 species and cultivars – are passed on return to the Visitor Centre, as well as the willow collection and a row of **Japanese Cherry** varieties.

STRATHCLYDE

39 Culzean

LOCATION **Off the A719, 12 miles (19 km) south-west of Ayr;** *Landranger Sheet 70, NS2310;* OPEN **(Country Park and garden) all year round, 9-sunset;** ADMISSION **pedestrians free; cars £2.**

Culzean Castle and Country Park stand dramatically on what used to be a bleak and windy stretch of coastline.

In the late-18th C this unprepossessing site was transformed, possibly by Robinson and Whyte, disciples of 'Capability' Brown, and in the late-19th C and early-20th C the 3rd Marquis of Ailsa established an extensive collection of exotics. These are to be found mainly in the Walled Garden, at the top of Silver Avenue, and in Happy Valley, slightly farther west – both areas being ideally sheltered for growing plants. The woodland walks around the Country Park are well worth exploring, as indeed is the interior of the fine castle, designed in 1777 by Robert Adam. It is built around a central tower, once a stronghold of the Kennedy family. The principal features of the interior are the round drawing room and the fine central staircase.

Best time of year
Spring, when the collection of tree rhododendrons in Happy Valley is in full bloom. Autumn colour, too, can be spectacular in this area of the Park, with the Orange Bark or Chilean Myrtle and **Persian Ironwood** vying for attention.

Other highlights
Maidenhair Tree from China and **Strawberry Tree** from Ireland and the Mediterranean occur in Fountain Court, adjacent to the castle. In Silver Avenue a *few* very large **Common Silver Firs** have survived the felling of 1977, as have Montezuma Pine, **Monterey Cypress** and a one hundred year-old **magnolia** *(M. × soulangiana)*.

Inside the Walled Garden look out for Chusan Palm, cucumber, **Indian Bean** and **Handkerchief Trees,** Japanese Red Cedar and **Cedar of Lebanon.** Out-side, there is a collection of young and mature **gum, Katsura** and Chilean Fire Tree, Patagonian Cypress and a form of Japanese Red Cedar.

Some of the finest mature exotic conifers are to be found in Happy Valley, including Western Hemlock and **Lawson Cypress. wellingtonias** also flourish.

40 Brodick Castle

LOCATION **Two miles (3 km) from Brodick Pier, Isle of Arran. Ferry from Ardrossan (one hour), bus from Pier;** *Landranger Sheet 69, NR 997380;* OPEN **(Country Park and garden) all year round: daily 9.30-sunset;** ADMISSION **(garden on-ly) £0.80, children £0.40.**

Brodick's position on the Isle of Arran, off Scotland's west coast, means that it has perfect conditions for growing trees: there are no climatic extremes, the garden and Country Park are sheltered, rainfall is heavy and the soil is excellent. Moreover, nowhere else is such a splendid Scottish island garden so accessible. Most of the garden has been planted since 1923, by the Duchess of Montrose and her son-in-law, John Boscawen, and the National Trust for Scotland. The informal grounds slope away from the Castle and formal walled garden down to the sea, and there are self-guided walks and nature trails.

Best time of year
Spring and early summer, when **magnolia,** and rhododendron, amongst other plants are at their best.

Other highlights
Down in the woodland, the Pond Garden displays some of the best exotics. There are Chinese Poplar; Chusan Palm from China; False, or Southern, Beech from South America; Black Bark Wattle from Australia; 'Leopoldii' Sycamore; Coffin Juniper; eucryphia and Snowdrop Tree. In the nearby woodland garden are **gum,** mimosa, Double Gean, or double white, **cherry** and **Common Silver Fir.**

With a little diligence, further specimens of some of these trees can be found elsewhere in the garden, but also look out for the excellent collection of willow as well as Cabbage Palm, Horse Chestnut, Grand Fir, Western Hemlock, **wellingtonia** and an im-mense **Cork Oak** by the entrance gate. There is also a 'Rheingold' **White Cedar** in the flower garden.

TAYSIDE

41 Branklyn Garden

LOCATION **In Perth on the Dundee road (A84);** *Landranger Sheet 58, NO1222;* OPEN **Mar to end-Oct: daily 9.30-sunset;** ADMISSION **£0.80, children £0.40.**

Despite its area of just one-and-three-quarter acres, this attractive garden, within the boundary of the City of Perth, is world-famous for its fine collection of alpine and peat garden and herbaceous plants.

It also boasts a number of interesting ornamental trees.

Branklyn was created by Mr and Mrs

John T. Renton in the 1920s and 1930s on the site of a former orchard.

Best time of year

Spring for a large Double Gean, a golden form of Downy Japanese Maple and **Smooth Japanese Maple;** late spring for **magnolia;** autumn for the multi-coloured foliage, particularly on many Japanese Maples (some fine specimens of *Acer palmatum* and *A. dissectum*).

Other highlights

Broad-leaves of note include a magnificent 60-year-old Orange-skinned Birch; Weeping Birch 'Crispa'; fastigiate hornbeam; beautiful Kashmir Rowan as well as *Sorbus vilmorinii* from China, **Snowbell Tree,** *Stuartia pseudocamelia* and *S. serrata*.

Amongst the conifer collection are found a curiously-shaped golden **Atlas Cedar,** a form of **Scots Pine** and a particularly fine pendent **Eastern Hemlock.**

GRAMPIAN

42 Crathes

LOCATION **On the road to Aberdeen (A93), 3 miles (5 km) east of Banchory;** *Landranger Sheets 38 or 45, NO9396;* OPEN **(garden and grounds only) all year: daily 9.30-sunset;** ADMISSION **(garden only) £0.80, children £0.40; (grounds only) £0.50, children £0.25.**

Crathes Castle is set in magnificent woodland typical of Royal Deeside. The extensive grounds, which include an enchanting Walled Garden, an artificial lake and sweeping lawns, contain many fine specimen trees. The property has been owned by the Burnett family for over 350 years and it was General Sir James Burnett who early this century redesigned the garden as we see it today and planted some unusual exotics. Five signposted woodland walks encourage the visitor to explore the grounds more fully.

Best time of year

Autumn colours along the approach drive and around the Castle are exceptionally beautiful and eye-catching.

Other highlights

One of the best stretches along which to view ornamental trees at Crathes is East Avenue, the main entrance drive. There you will find numerous **maples,** including **Cappadocian,** Hers's and Norway Maple, **Turkey Oak,** 'Dawyck' Beech, **Tree of Heaven** and Coffin Tree (near the lake). Among the exotic conifers are **Brewer's Weeping Spruce, Swamp Cypress** and Himalayan and **Colorado White Fir.** Another excellent but smaller area of interest is halfway along the North Trail.

Near the Castle, particularly to the south-west, are such exotics as **Coast** and **Dawn Redwood,** Monterey Pine, **Noble Fir, Monkey Puzzle, Hupeh Rowan** and **Maidenhair Tree.** In the Walled Garden look out for **Japanese Cherry, Paper-bark Maple, Handkerchief Tree,** an old **Indian Bean Tree** and an ancient Portuguese Laurel. Beside the back road are numerous **firs** of note – Forrest's, **Beautiful, Cauca-sian,** California Red and Santa Lucia – as well as **Japanese Red Cedar** and Northern Japanese Hemlock.

Another notable area is along the West Drive, where you should see Oregon Maple, Antarctic Beech, Chinese Varnish Tree, Western Hemlock and **deodar.** Caroline's Garden, nearby, includes Japanese Umbrella Pine, **Snake-bark Maple** and Dombey's False, or Southern, Beech; scattered generally around the grounds are also specimens of **Common Lime,** Grey Willow, Weeping Elm and both Grand and **Common Silver Fir.**

---

43 Drum Castle

LOCATION **Off the road from Aberdeen to Banchory (A93), 3 miles (5 km) west of Peterculter;** *Landranger Sheet 38, NJ7900;* OPEN **(grounds only) all year round: daily 9.30-sunset;** ADMISSION **(grounds only) by donation.**

Drum Castle attracts tree lovers from all over the world who are anxious to visit the magnificent arboretum located in the parkland close to the Castle. Here there are literally hundreds of rare species some mature specimens (mainly conifers), while many others are recently planted.

Best time of year

Spring and early summer blossoms are beautiful at Drum, aided by collections of **magnolia,** flowering **cherry** and ornamental apple. Unusual trees producing memorable blooms include **Judas, Foxglove, Locust** and **Snowbell**

Trees, Yellow Buckeye, **Manna Ash** and 'Vossii' laburnum. Autumn foliage colour is also attractive, the large collections of **maple** and **rowan** being especially prominent at this season. **Japanese Red Cedar, Scarlet Oak,** Roble Beech, raoul and **Katsura Tree** also contribute to the spectacle.

Other highlights

Conifers abound in the arboretum at Drum, and most are fine mature specimens. Of the mature trees look out for **Delavay's** and Veitch's **Silver Fir** and Grand Fir; blue and ordinary **Atlas Cedar; deodar,** Patagonian and **Monterey Cypress,** cultivars of **Sawara Cypress; morinda, Oriental,** Colorado and **Brewer's Weeping Spruce;** Japanese Umbrella, **Western Yellow** and Monterey **Pine;** Western and **Mountain Hemlock, hiba,** Pencil Cedar and **wellingtonia.**

Notable young exotic conifers include **Spanish, Grecian,** Chinese and **Colorado White Fir;** Cultivars of **Lawson Cypress;** and **Stone,** Mexican White and Japanese White **Pine.**

Among the outstanding young broadleaves are **Indian Bean Tree, Black Walnut** and **Tulip Tree** from North America; Weeping Willow-leaved Pear, Common Walnut and **Black Mulberry** from central Asia; **Maidenhair Tree** from China; False, or Southern, Beech from South America; **Cider Gum** from Australia; and many rare birches including Yellow, Paper-bark and Erman's Birch. There are also mature specimens of Golden Downy Japanese Maple, **Handkerchief Tree,** Copper Beech, Farges's Holly and Irish Yew.

44 Haddo House

LOCATION **Off the B9005 between Ellon and Methlick, 19 miles (30 km) north of Aberdeen;** *Landranger Sheet 30, NJ8634;* OPEN **(garden and Country Park) all year round: daily 9.30-sunset;** ADMISSION **(garden and Country Park); no charge for admission.**

Many of the beautiful mature trees at Haddo were planted in the early-19th C by the 4th Earl of Aberdeen, who was also responsible for designing the panorama of parkland and woodland. He was much influenced by Sir Uvedale Price and Sir William Payne Knight, and the park area today, with its network of paths, trees and its wildlife, is a fitting tribute to the Earl's work and foresight. The woodlands surrounding the garden and in the Country Park contain a wide variety of broad-leaved trees and conifers, including some fine exotics, which can best be appreciated by following the tree trail.

Best time of year

Worth visiting at any time of year.

Other highlights

Double Gean, or Wild Cherry, on the west side; two magnificent **wellingtonias,** more than one hundred years old, on the east side, plus another **wellingtonia** close to some fine Copper Beeches and **Common Limes** (in a short avenue) on the south side of the garden.

In the Country Park itself are a mature Cockscomb Beech, Norway Maple, Purple sycamore and Horse Chestnut. Exotic conifers include **Lawson Cypress, Monkey Puzzle,** Lodgepole Pine, **Noble Fir** and Western Hemlock.

ULSTER

Lough Neagh

Belfast

46

47 45

COUNTY DOWN

45 Rowallane

LOCATION **Eleven miles (18 km) south-east of Belfast, west of the A7; *Landranger J409575;* OPEN Apr, July to end-Oct: Mon to Fri 9-6, Sat and Sun 2-6. May and June: Mon to Fri 9-9, Sat and Sun 2-6. Nov to end-Mar: Mon to Fri only 9-4.30; *Closed 25 and 26 Dec, 1 Jan;* ADMISSION Apr to June £1, children £0.50; July to end-Oct £0.75, children £0.40. Nov to Mar £0.50, children £0.25.**

Rowallane is a plantsman's garden, principally designed and developed by one person, Hugh Armytage Moore in the first half of the 20th C. It has a relatively low number of cultivars and hybrids, because many of its trees were derived from plant hunting expeditions, by the 19th-C explorer Henry Wilson, amongst others. Its Asiatic Collection is strong, and there is an arboretum. Autumns are late, and mild weather often lasts into November and December in this part of the country, so conditions are suited to tender plants at Rowallane.

Best time of year

Although spring is beautiful here, the autumn pageant of coloured leaves is also memorable.

Other highlights

Rowallane has such a wide variety of rare trees that only a few can be mentioned here. False Beech *(Nothofagus)* is probably the most notable speciality. Ten taxa are cultivated, with both South American and Australasian species growing equally well. There are also numerous different species of **rowan,** *Malus* and cultivated **cherry,** including **Sargent's Cherry** from Japan. *Podocarpus* is yet another speciality, a plum-fruited yew over 30 ft (9 m) tall. **Magnolia** is not as abundant as might be expected for an Irish garden, but there are still 18 taxa represented, by far the most important being the rare *M. dawsoniana* from China, which is in the outer Walled Garden.

Nearby, in the Pleasure Gardens, are numerous exotic conifers including **Tiger Tail Spruce** from Japan, **Monkey Puzzle** from South America; **Mountain Hemlock;** numerous cultivars of **Lawson Cypress** (including glaucous and gold-coloured forms); Monterey Pine; **wellingtonia** and the very rare **Eastern Hemlock** – all these last five coming from North America. You will also see Indian Horse Chestnut and **Caucasian Wing-nut.**

In the arboretum are found a steely-blue **juniper,** a late-flowering hawthorn from eastern North America *(Crataegus cordata),* a fine grafted birch *(Betula ermanii),* a very tall Snowdrop Tree, an evergreen spindle and specimens, such as *Malus hupehensis, Prunus litigiosa* and

Docynia rufifolia grown from the original Wilson seed.

Other prominent trees include **Snake-bark Maple, Smooth** and downy **Japanese Maple,** Norway Maple, **Handkerchief Tree** and a group of different **gum** species. Among the exotic conifers look out for **Nootka Cypress, Brewer's Weeping Spruce, White Cedar** (in three cultivars differing in colour), a form of **Colorado White Fir, Delavay's Silver Fir** and Veitch's Silver Fir – all from North America. One of the most impressive trees of all is a graceful Mexican White Pine by the drive.

46 Mount Stewart

LOCATION **On the Belfast to Portaferry road (A20), 5 miles (8 km) south-east of Newtonards; *Landranger J555701;* OPEN (garden only) Apr: Sat and Sun 2-6. May to end-Jun, Sept to end-Oct: Tues to Sun 2-6. Jul to Aug: Tues to Sun 12-8; ADMISSION (garden and temple only) £1, children £0.50.**

Mount Stewart is arguably the most complete garden property owned by the National Trust: it includes almost every style of gardening and supports an incomparable plant collection. The design and flora are largely the work of the 7th Marchioness of Londonderry, who came to live at Mount Stewart in 1921. Owing to its position between two sea loughs and its proximity to the Gulf Stream, many tender trees grow in this garden. Southern Hemisphere species dominate, especially those from

Australasia and South America. The lururiant growth of the flora, made possible by the mild climate, disguises the garden's youth and produces an almost sub-tropical effect. Microclimates exist and some of the tenderest trees are found on south-facing Cemetery Hill, north of the lake.

Best time of year
Spring, when the garden is awash with blooms including Kowhai Tree from New Zealand, **magnolia** and many cultivars of ornamental **cherry.** Sycamore 'Brilliantissimum' and 'Prinz Handjery' also provide memorable spring foliage colour. Autumn colour is surprisingly fine, too, especially around the lake. Apart from **Sargent's Cherry, Katsura Tree** and some rare birches, **maple** abounds, particularly purple-leaved **Smooth Japanese Maple.**

Other highlights
Other major exotic tree specialities at Mount Stewart are **gum,** for example southern blue gum, **Snow Gum** from Tasmania, **Cider Gum,** and many more rarities; also *Cordyline,* including New Zealand Cabbage Tree and *C. indivisa.*

A huge, rugged Monterey Pine dominates the prospect north of the house. Nearby are also found **Lucombe, Cork, Holm** and **Turkey Oak;** Yellow and Cherry Birch; **wellingtonia** and **Common silver Fir.** Nearer the house stand some topiary pieces of Sweet Bay.

Tall trees dominate west of the house in Lily Wood but you should also find **Dwarf Fan-palm,** Chusan Palm and an evergreen False Beech from Chile.

Nearby, in the Memorial Glade, is Japanese Alder. Towards the shore of Strangford Lough grow two of the most remarkable conifers at Mount Stewart: *Phyllocladus* from New Zealand; and two towering Irish yews, which stand sentinel by the south front of the house.

Other exotics of note scattered around the garden include forms or cultivars of Oriental Plane and White Willow; **spruce,** poplar, beech and an attractively barked birch from China; raoul, Antarctic Beech and a 55-ft (17-m) eucryphia from South America; mimosa and Sydney Golden Wattle from Australia; and Paper-bark Birch and orange-crimson Barked Madrona from North America. Also look out for **deodar, Atlas Cedar** and **Cedar of Lebanon, Lawson Cypress** 'Columnaris', **Grecian** and Himalayan **Fir, Monterey Cypress** and an impressive 35-ft (11-m) *Cupressus cashmeriana* from Bhutan.

---

47 Castle Ward

LOCATION Off the road to Strangford (A25), 7 miles (11 km) northeast of Downpatrick; *Landranger J752494;* **OPEN (grounds only) all year round: daily 9-sunset; ADMISSION (grounds only) £0.80 per car.**

Castle Ward is picturesquely situated on the south shore of Strangford Lough, where it benefits from the Gulf Stream. Most of the landscaping was carried out between 1720 and 1750 by Judge Michael Ward, who designed the lower garden, including Temple Water around his Queen Anne house, which no

longer exists. In the 19th C and 20th C, there was much overlay planting in this area, which is close to the Lough. The pinetum was planted following the building the the late-18th C of the present house considerably further south.

Best time of year
In autumn Castle Ward comes alive with vibrant multi-coloured foliage from honey-locust; American **Red Oak** and **Silver Maple** from North America; Roble Beech and raoul from Chile, and keaki from Japan.

Other highlights
Exotic conifers of note west of the house include **Incense Cedar; Noble** and Californian red **Fir; deodar; Lawson Cypress** cultivars; **Smooth Arizona Cypress;** glaucous form of Douglas Fir; **wellingtonia** and Western Red Cedar – all from North America. Also present in this area are **Hinoki Cypress** from Japan; Chilean **Incense Cedar** and Patagonian Cypress from South America; **Serbian Spruce;** Chinese Thuja, and some fine examples of Irish yew.

To the east of the house look out for blue **Atlas Cedar, hiba** and Monterey Pine. Ballycutter Avenue southwards to Ballycutter Lodge is predominantly broad-leaved, but **Common Silver Fir** and **Sawara Cypress** also occur. Broad-leaves growing in this area include **Holm** and **Turkey Oak,** copper beech, whitebeam, **Downy Japanese Maple,** Oriental Plane and Golden Willow.

Walking from the house northwards along Laurel Walk to Strangford Lough, you should find summit and **Japanese**

Red Cedar, **Lawson** and **Monterey Cypress** and **Monkey Puzzle**.

The area surrounding Temple Water, well north of the present house, is where most of the interesting broad-leaves are to be seen. There are **Silver** and **Silver Pendent Lime; London Plane; Hungarian Oak; Caucasian Wing-nut; Handkerchief Tree** from China; **Tree of Heaven** and evergreen false beech from Chile; **Black Walnut; Tulip Tree;** and yellow buck-eye from North America. Also present are **Atlas Cedar, Cedar of Lebanon, Stone** and **Bhutan Pine, Coast Redwood, Swamp Cypress** and **Western Hemlock**.

REPUBLIC OF IRELAND

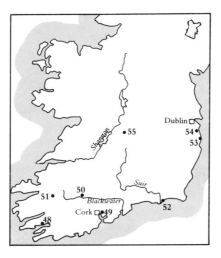

CO CORK

48 Ilnacullin

LOCATION **On Garinish Island in the sheltered harbour of Glengarriff in Bantry Bay;** OPEN **Mar to end-Oct: daily 10-6;** ADMISSION **IR£1.20.**

Small island garden of great beauty known to horticulturists and lovers of trees all around the world. Contains extensive plantings of conifers as well as tree rhododendrons, acacia, **gum, magnolia** and juniper, amongst numerous other trees.

49 Fota

LOCATION **Fota Island, Cork harbour;** OPEN **Apr to end-Sept: Mon to Fri 11-6. Sun 2-6. Oct to end-Mar: Sun and public holidays 2-6;** ADMISSION **IR£1.50, children IR£0.50.**

The arboretum contains many old trees dating from 1850. Specimens include **Japanese Red Cedar, Coast Redwood, Atlas Cedar** and Huon Pine; two podocarps, *Podocarpus salignus* and *P. totara,* also deserve mention. There are two fine examples of *Magnolia grandiflora* in the Walled Garden and a large multi-stemmed Cabbage Tree.

50 Annes Grove Gardens

LOCATION **One mile (1.5 km) north of Castletownroche, which is on the main Fermoy/Mallow/Killarney road;** OPEN **Easter to end-Sept: Mon to Fri 10-5. Sun 1-6;** ADMISSION **IR£1.50, children IR£1.**

Handkerchief Tree is grown in association with white-flowering **magnolia**. In the River Garden autumn colour is provided by **Katsura Tree** and the North American trees **Swamp Cypress** and Yellow Buckeye. Growing in a woodland area amongst rhododendrons are specimens of **Lawson Cypress** 'Wissellii', *Juniperus recurva* 'Castlewellan' and **Dawn Redwood**.

CO KERRY

51 Muckross Gardens

LOCATION **In the Bourn-Vincent National Park at Killarney;** OPEN **at all times;** ADMISSION **free.**

In these gardens are fine mature **Tree of Heaven, Katsura Tree,** Cabbage Tree, **Tulip Tree, magnolia, crab,** false beech, **Persian Ironwood** and several kinds of **maple, gum,** eucryphia and rowan. The range of exotic and less hardy trees is constantly increased. The screening woodlands include specimens of **Coast Redwood,** Monterey Pine and Western Hemlock.

CO WEXFORD

52 John F. Kennedy Memorial Arboretum

LOCATION **Eight miles (13 km) south of New Ross on R733 (LI59) to Hook Head; OPEN Apr and Sept: daily 10-6.30. May to Aug: 10-8.30. Oct to Mar: 10-5; ADMISSION Cars IR£1.**

This internationally known arboretum is a young (opened in 1968) comprehensive collection of trees and shrubs at present amounting to 4,500 taxa planted in family groups. Of particular interest is the ericaceous bed with 500 different rhododendrons, a collection of 100 **maples** and a collection of 300 species and varieties of slow-growing conifers.

There are in addition 190 plots of interesting forestry trees.

CO WICKLOW

53 Mount Usher Gardens

LOCATION **At Ashford on main Dublin to Wicklow road, 28 miles** (45 km) from Dublin; OPEN **Apr to end-Sept: Mon to Sat 10.30-6. Sun 2-6; ADMISSION IR£1.50, children IR£0.60.**

Southern Hemisphere trees such as false beech, **gum,** and *Athrotaxis* thrive in this garden. A specimen of Montezuma Pine, planted in 1909, is one of the tallest in these islands. Unusual conifers include Chinese fir, *Dacrydium cupressinum* and *Tsuga dumosa.* Among the maples are specimens of **Paper-bark Maple,** Coral-bark Maple and *Acer henryii.* Maximowixz's Birch stands by the river bank.

54 Powerscourt Gardens

LOCATION **On the outskirts of the village of Enniskerry, 13 miles (20 km) south of Dublin; OPEN Easter to end-Oct: 10-5.30; ADMISSION IR£1.60, children IR£0.80.**

There are many notable conifers in the collection, including **Monterey Cypress,** planted in 1867, Western Red Cedar, *Pinus coulteri,* **Hinoki Cypress** and Monterey Pine. an avenue of **Monkey Puzzle** creates an impressive garden feature. Broad-leaves of note are **Caucasian Wing-nut,** Blue Gum and *Nothofagus betuloides,* a false, or southern, beech.

CO OFFALY

55 Birr Castle

LOCATION **A few minutes' walk from the town centre of Birr; OPEN** all year round: daily 9-1 and 2-6 (or duck, if earlier); ADMISSION IR£2, children IR£1.50.

There are many old specimens including of Caucasian Lime, which date from the 18th C. Earlier this century representative collections of **oak,** birch, thorn and **maple** were planted. In the Formal Garden are very large examples of **Tree of Heaven, wellingtonia** and tall box hedges. There are many **magnolias** in the garden including *Magnolia dawsoniana, M. kobus, M. sargentiana* and *M. delavayii;* also **cherries** and **crabs.** The tallest tree is Grey Poplar, almost 120 ft (40 m) tall, while another poplar, Chinese Necklace Tree, is about 60 ft (20 m).

Glossary

Annual ring Ring of wood laid down in stem and branches of tree or shrub during one growing season.
Arboretum A botanical tree garden.

Branchlet Small branch, between branch and twig in size.
Bud scale Scale that covers and protects a developing leaf.

Cambium Layer of living cells just under bark and at growing tips of shoots and roots, from which new growth develops.
Carr A copse on boggy ground on fenland.
Compound Term describing leaf that consists of several LEAFLETS.
Cone axis Central core of cone.
Cone scale Woody structure rising from CONE AXIS, enclosing developing seeds.
Coniferous Term describing tree that bears cones.
Coppicing Cutting of woody stem at ground level to encourage growth of several stems from one root system.
Cross-fertilisation Fertilisation of the OVULE of one individual plant by the pollen from another.
Crown Branches and upper part of trunk of tree.
Cultivar Variation of a SPECIES arising in cultivation, and propagated for some unusual characteristic such as leaf colour or shape.

Deciduous Term describing tree or shrub that retains its leaves for one growing season only, dropping them before the following winter.

Entire Term describing leaf without lobes, teeth or other indentations in margin.

Family Large group of similar plants, made up of several genera (see GENUS).

Genus Group of closely related plants distinct enough not to interbreed. Usually consists of several SPECIES. Plural: genera.
Grafting Artificial union of the aerial parts of one plant with another.

Hanging wood Woodland growing up steep slope.
Hardy Tolerant of adverse conditions of climate and soil.
Heartwood Dead wood at centre of tree trunk or branch, no longer water-conducting tissue but providing structural support.
Hybrid Offspring of CROSS-FERTILISATION.

Indigenous Native.

Layering Term describing the development of a new individual plant from a branch or stem that has rooted into the ground.
Leaflet Leaf-shaped subdivision of a COMPOUND leaf.
Lenticel Small pore in bark.

Lobe Rounded indentation on leaf margin.

Native A species which is thought to have reached Britain since the Ice Age without the aid of man.

Opposite Term used of buds or leaves of broad-leaved trees that are arranged in pairs on the twig.
Ovule Unfertilised, rudimentary seed of a flowering plant.

Perfect Term describing a flower with both male and female parts.
Persistent Term describing part of a plant that does not fall, wither or disappear, as is usual with the some parts of other plants.
Pinetum ARBORETUM planted with coniferous trees.
Pinnate Term used of leaf completely subdivided into several LEAFLETS ranged along either side of midrib.
Pollarding Lopping of the topmost branches of a tree to encourage shoots to arise all at the same level.
Pulvinus Base of a leaf-stalk: the swollen part of a shoot from which a leaf arises.

Sapwood Living wood in tree trunk, through which water from soil is conducted up a tree.
Sepal Scale, similar to BUD SCALE, but covering and protecting the developing flower.

Short shoot Shoot which extends only a little each year.
Simple Term describing a leaf that is not divided into LEAFLETS.
Species Group of plants similar in all respects and able to interbreed.
Springwood Inner part of ANNUAL RING, formed early in growing season, consisting of thin-walled vessels for conducting water.
Stipule Leaf-like growth on stem at base of leaf-stalk, often in pairs.
Sucker Shoot arising directly from a root, or at base of a stem.
Summerwood Outer part of ANNUAL RING, formed during middle and later part of growing season, consisting of thick-walled vessels for conducting water up the stem.

Tap root Main downward-growing root of seedling.
Taxa (plural of taxon) general term for any unit of classification, be it form, variety, species, genus, family and so on; mostly used when speaking of several such categories at the same time.
Tooth One of a series of small, regular points on a leaf margin.

Variety Variation of a SPECIES arising in the wild, usually differing in only one characteristic, such as colour or leaf shape.

Index

TREES

A
Ash, Manna 48

B
Bean tree, Indian 16

C
Catalpa, Yellow 16
Cedar, Atlas 59
  Incense 94
  Japanese Red 85
  of Lebanon 58
  White 93
Cherry, Japanese 25
  Sargent's 24
Crab Apple 21
Cypress, Hinoki 92
  Lawson 89
  Monterey 88
  Nootka 90
  Sawara 91
  Smooth Arizona 87
  Swamp 72

D
deodar 57

E
Elder, Box 54

F
Fan-palm, Dwarf 56
Fir, Beautiful 62
  Caucasian 61
  Colorado White 63
  Common Silver 60
  Delavay's Silver 66
  Forrest's 66
  Grecian 65
  Low's 63
  Noble 67
  Spanish 64
Foxglove Tree 17

G
Gum, Cider 31
  Snow 32
  Sweet 39

H
Handkerchief Tree 18
Hemlock, Eastern 69
  Mountain 68
hiba 95

I
Ironwood, Persian 22

J
Judas Tree 12
Juniper, Chinese 86

K
Katsura Tree 13

L
Lime, Common 14
  Silver 15
  Silver Pendent 15
Locust Tree 52

M
magnolia 23
Maidenhair Tree 55
Maple, Cappadocian 33
  Paper-bark 47
  Red 34
  Silver 35
  Smooth Japanese 37
  Downy Japanese 37
  Snake-bark 36
medlar 26
Monkey Puzzle 73
morinda 78
Mulberry, Black 19
Mulberry, White 29

O
Oak, Cork 27
  Holm 28
  Hungarian 44
  Lucombe 45
  Pin 43
  Red 41
  Scarlet 42
  Turkey 46

P
Palm, Chusan 56

Pine, Arolla 82
  Bhutan 81
  Jeffrey's 80
  Macedonian 83
  Stone 79
  Western Yellow 80
Plane, London 38
  Oriental 39

R
Redwood, Coast 70
  Dawn 71
Rowan, Hupeh 53

S
Snowbell Tree 29
Spruce, Brewster's Weeping 77
  Oriental 76
  Serbian 75
  Tiger Tail 74
Strawberry Tree 20

T
Thuja, Chinese 93
Tree of Heaven 50
Tulip Tree 40

W
Walnut, Black 49
wellingtonia 84
Willow, Golden Weeping 30
Wing-nut, Caucasian 51

SITES

A
Annes Grove Gardens 123
Arlington Court 101
Attingham Park 110

B
Belton 113-14
Beningbrough Hall 115
Birr Castle 124
Blickling Hall 114
Bodnant Garden 107-8
Branklyn Garden 118-19
Brodick Castle 118

C
Castle Ward 122-3
Chirk Castle 108
Cliveden 106
Clumber Park 113
Cotehele 99
Cragside 116-17
Crathes 119
Croft Castle 109-10
Culzean 117-18

D
Dudmaston 110
Dunham Massey 112
Drum Castle 119-20

F
Felbrigg Hall 114-15
Fota 123

G
Greys Court 108-9

H
Haddo House 120
Hardwick Hall 112-13

I
Ilnacullin 123

K
Kennedy, John F., Memorial
   Arboretum 124

Killerton 100
Knighthayes Court 100-1

L
Lacock Abbey 102
Lanhydrock 98-9

M
Montacute 101
Mount Stewart 121-2
Mount Usher Gardens 124
Muckross Gardens 124

N
Nymans Garden 104

P
Petworth 103-4
Plas Newydd 107
Powerscourt Gardens 124
Powis Castle 106-7

R
Rowallane 121

S
Saltram 99-100
Sheffield Park Garden 104-5
Shugborough 111
Stourhead 102-3
Studley Royal 115-16

T
Tatton Park 111-12
Threave Garden 117
Trelissick 98

V
Vyne, The 103

W
Waddesdon Manor 109
Wallington 116
Winkworth Arboretum 105-6

Acknowledgements

The editor and publishers would like to thank the following for their invaluable help in compiling information for this book:

Dr T.W. Wright, Adviser on Conservation and Woodlands, The National Trust.

Staff of the National Trust, in particular head gardeners, regional foresters, regional information officers, administrators and land agents who supplied information and answered queries.

Graeme Morison, Michael Blacklock and Judy Aitken of the National Trust for Scotland.

Staff of the National Trust for Scotland, especially principals, ranger-naturalists and resident representatives, who supplied information and answered queries.

Richard Webb, An Taisce (National Trust for Ireland).

Sara Shepley, Centre Manager, Witley Common Information Centre, the National Trust, for her feature on basic fieldcraft.

Editorial and design
Researched and written by Joanna Chisholm; assistant editor Rosemary Dawe; designed by Arthur Brown; map on page 96 by Line and Line.

ORNAMENTAL TREES
is based on the Reader's Digest Field Guide to the Trees and Shrubs of Britain to which the following made major contributions:

CONSULTANTS AND AUTHORS
Esmond Harris, B.Sc., Dip. For., F.I. For., Director, The Royal Forestry Society of England, Wales and Northern Ireland
Jeanette Harris, B.Sc.

ARTISTS

Dick Bonson	Charles Raymond
Brian Delf	Derek Rodgers
Shirley Felts	Jim Russell
Ian Garrard	David Salariya
Nick Hall	Ann Savage
Delyth Jones	Bruce Whatley

The publishers would also like to thank The Royal Forestry Society of England, Wales and Northern Ireland for its valuable and expert assistance in the preparation of this book

RNNB–16–009